Grief's
Hermitage

Grief's Hermitage

A book of comfort and consolation for the bereaved

JOSEPHINE GRIFFITHS

Because of the dynamic nature of the Internet, any web addresses or links contained in
this book may have changed since publication and may no longer be valid. The views
expressed in this work are solely those of the author and do not necessarily reflect the
views of the publisher and the publisher hereby disclaims any responsibility for them.

The author of this book does not dispense medical advice or prescribe the use of any
technique as a form of treatment for physical, emotional, or medical problems without
the advice of a physician, either directly or indirectly. The intent of the author(s) is only
to offer information of a general nature to help you in your quest for emotional and
spiritual well-being and expression. In the event you use any of the information in this
book for yourself, which is your constitutional right, the author(s) and the publisher
assume no responsibility for your actions.

 A catalogue record for this
book is available from the
NATIONAL LIBRARY National Library of Australia
OF AUSTRALIA

ISBN: 978-0-9579701-9-9 (paperback)
ISBN: 978-0-6481697-0-3 (hardback)

DEDICATION

For Bernard
And for the many beautiful friends and relations
'on another shore and in a greater light'.

CONTENTS

INTRODUCTION

It is nearly eighteen years since my husband, Bernard, died.
We had had a long, interesting and happy marriage some of which
was spent in parish work within the Anglican Church. He had two
parishes before going into hospital chaplaincy, the position he held
until his death. His last year was one of declining health, but his
death was still a very great shock from which it took a long time
to recover.

The idea of *Grief's Hermitage* was first imagined in the early years of
my grieving. I thought a good deal about writing it and even made
occasional attempts at starting. Looking back I see those attempts
as protective and projective, a way of ordering the chaos, thinking
that by writing, directing my agony into a useful channel I might
find some surcease of sorrow. Now, more than a decade later, I am
able at last to embrace the challenge and the pleasure of compiling
an anthology or common-place book for anyone who wants
something to dip into now and then when sadness is looking for the
odd clue or a momentary balm.

The pieces are not arranged to be read progressively; grief is the
only organising principle. To arrange the material according to 'the
stages of grief' model would go against the grain of my inclination

and my experience. I have always been like that. When I was having babies I never wanted to know about how or in what order I should expect the process of delivery to take place. Even at that tender age I had a strong sense that to be waiting and watching for the things to go on in the right order would somehow militate against my own experience. I knew myself at least that well: I would be wondering if I was getting it right and so miss the experience. This birth was my experience, unique and unrepeatable, so it was with grief.

One thing I had observed in my reading, long before there was any need for concern, was that different researchers gave the grieving process differing normal durations. Some gave it in months, some in years, two or three, and one writer (I cannot remember who it was) said eight years was not abnormal or unnatural. This stuck in my mind. Seven years and ten months after B left I woke up one morning feeling like I was together again. The grief was still there, but it was me grieving; I was no longer a left over fragment of a once viable couple.

Many people have surely found the stages of grief that have been defined by wonderful and caring specialists to be of immense comfort, just as many, perhaps most, mothers-to-be feel safer and more assured if they know what's going to happen and in what order, as they give birth for the first time. I have explained my variance from that norm so that the lack of progression in this book makes sense and also because I think there are people like me who find being sized up to a given model agonising and oppressive. People who like the model do not feel sized up or oppressed by it; people who are not comfortable with fitting a given can feel odd and so add to their already overstrained emotions the anxiety about what they should or should not be feeling. Having been a Misfit all my life I am sensitive to the distortions that mis-fittery can bring about in times of stress.

Each cause for grief is unique, just as each birth is unique. Of course there are similarities, but to the person grieving, as to the new mother, the uniqueness of their experience carries by far the greater importance. Grief is also chaotic and random, even after years have passed one can still, out of the blue, feel as though the beloved has only just gone. Grief, like love, partakes of the nature of eternity and the obvious, though often ignored fact about eternity is the absence of time. We humans cannot really get with the idea of the absence of time but in love, and in grief, we can experience timelessness even while we do not understand it. Both states can temporarily carry us beyond our ordinary human limitations, but in them we do not observe ourselves for we are too absorbed by the experience.

Reflecting on the experience is mainly what this book is about in the hope that through the words of poets and writers both ancient and modern we may find, even perhaps in the most unlikely places, thoughts that can enliven, enlighten, comfort and console. I hope too that we may occasionally find laughter.

Much of this book is from the perspective of the loss of a primary loved one, but, of course, we can grieve for many different people and purposes and for our pets that become so entangled in our emotional lives.

As I write this I am suffering grief over the death of a very dear friend of almost fifty years, and the death of a dear family pet.

This makes me aware that grieving for friends or pets can stir us deeply and set up its own confusions. Over our friends we can feel we don't 'have the right' to make a fuss, or be overt in our grief in case we look ostentatious or as if, somehow, we are encroaching on someone else's emotional territory. So much of grief brings us into conflict with what other people may think is appropriate. Maybe they don't think negatively but our inner sense that they might can contort the straightforward expression of what we feel.

This is when in retiring, at least in attitude, to our hermitage we can allow ourselves to feel the reality of great sadness without having it judged or thought to be judged by anyone else. Sadness, grief, the sense of loss are real feelings and do not need to be condemned. What we feel is neither good nor bad, it is simply what we feel, an expression of our own individual emotional life which does not have to meet any pre-conceived pattern of appropriate responses.

It has been a long struggle as to whether I should include in this book something of my own experience, *as I experienced it*. It is a comparatively easy thing to write retrospectively, but inevitably that is coloured by the passage of time, and pain in recollection, spoken of from a distance of more than a decade, will not have the reality level, the poignancy of the actual experience. Why should I consider sharing these agonies and ecstasies? When I conceived of writing this book it was because I believed it was worth the effort to bring some kind of consolation, through my words and the words of poets and other thinkers, to people in the time of their acute bereavement. The bits and pieces from my journal give a very real account of the kinds of ups and downs, and downs, that one goes through at the loss of a loved one.

Some of the experiences cannot usefully be shared with one's loved ones, who are also grieving and don't need anything more to add to their distress. These expressions are, nevertheless, the kind of thoughts that one goes through and the fact that someone else has put them into words might be a comfort, as though to say, "Look, that's how everyone feels from time to time, it is okay. It is so horrible to feel that way but it is okay."

The second reason for including actual experiences is really at the heart of this book. I have always believed in the continuation of life after death and that love is stronger than death. The days following B's death tested these beliefs to the utmost, but did prove to me that they were well-founded. This material could well be of value to other people who are grieving. The words I wrote through those dark days catalogue the certainty and the doubt. There were days when I not only believed in his abiding presence and love but I experienced it; there were days when I wondered if it was all a load of wish-fulfilment as the doubters would affirm. I know that there were many, many desperate times when I would have given everything to have had even a momentary sense of his presence, and it didn't come. When he did come it was always a shock, not when I was looking for it, hoping for it, begging for it. I had no say in the matter of his being there; if it were merely wish-fulfilment I would have had more control and probably given myself more constant comfort. The quality of these visitations baffled my imagination and was distinctly different in kind from memories or images conjured up by my conscious mind.

Perhaps in the sharing of these experiences readers may be encouraged to believe in the possibility of a continued connection with a loved one. The experts and researchers in the field seem to agree that the onus of establishing such a connection lies very strongly with the one still living in the flesh. This may read like an argument on the side of the 'wish-fulfilment' viewpoint, but it is just common psychological sense. What we believe about the continuation of our communication to a large extent determines how it will be, not because we make it happen in our minds, but because our beliefs will determine whether or not we are open to the overtures that may come.

I remember hearing a man sharing his experiences of his departed wife and how loving and beautiful it was for a brief time; then he had a dream, which he recounted. In the dream he saw his wife and he knew that she was saying good-bye and that he would never experience her presence again. As he recounted the dream I couldn't help thinking that the imagery might as well have been interpreted in the opposite way but the dreamer, in consciousness, did not believe in the possibility of communication with the departed in any shape or form. He was surprised that it had happened but knew that it could not last, so how could it?

This present work takes the opposite view. In this somewhat eclectic gathering of short writings you will find pieces from a variety of authors who hold different views of life and death, but none of the 'once you are dead you are dead' category. There are many, many books available; some works of consolation; some arguing for the continuance of life beyond death; some promoting a strongly traditional Christian viewpoint. It is a wide open field and we have to take care as we make our choices.

While I do not want to impose a specifically religious template, I am clearly writing for people who have some sort of belief in life being more than is admitted by scientific materialism. Love, beauty, art, grief all point to ranges of experience that cannot be encompassed in a purely materialistic world. Speaking of the Divine does not commit one to a Christian view of God or the After-Life. It is important to keep the language fluid for we all make our own interpretation of the symbols, in line with our personal faith. Some of the ancient writers used 'Energy' as a term to cover the Unseen and, in our time, given what we have learnt from quantum physics, maybe that is a really good word to use.

For some people the specifically religious point of view will bring solace, so I have given a chapter especially to Christian writers. Other people do not identify with that approach but find in the poets a voice that they can hear. There is a good selection of poems covering all shades of experience of loss, of despair, of gratitude and hope.

I count myself fortunate to have had so many wise guides and mentors in the books that I have read over the years. In no way did that richness cover or assuage the pain of loss but I did at least 'have somewhere to go'; resources to apply to when I needed something to counteract the deadly silence. It is my hope that this collection will provide a similar resource for people who are in a place where their normal patterns of focus, interest or engagement are totally interrupted by grief and they need something to hold on to.

WHY HERMITAGE?

Hermit and hermitage are ideas with a very long history. The ideas carry layers of meaning and symbolism that connect so well to the experience of grieving that they can comfort and inspire us to see, if not purpose, at least some beauty in what we are going through. 'Hermitage' is a good word for the state grief brings us to, simple and expressive, but with great depth and resonance to enrich and support us through these painful and tender times.

Genuine hermits are quite rare these days; that is, genuine in the sense of the formal dedication of a life set apart, sustained by God and by the gifts of the faithful. However, we do understand what it means sometimes to need to be apart. Very early on when I was bereaved I came to see that grief can impose internally a kind of hermit-like situation. One is sealed off from ordinary life, even if to outsiders we seem to behave normally.

No matter how convincing and safe our persona may be, inwardly we are cut off from everyday experience. A modern dictionary definition of hermitage is a place "to be insulated or protected from outside influences". That is what often comes about on the inside, because we have a great need to be protected from outside influences. Even if we have suffered grief before, this will be different. We have to be separate to allow time to discover this new configuration of our being, since some part of us has fled. Going apart we may still be in the midst of work, family and friends; our hermitage is a place of the heart.

Insulated or protected from outside influences may be the best we can have. As we are not that clear about what we need ourselves nobody else can know for us and all the well-meaning helpfulness, jollying, encouraging, sympathising or attempts at distraction are outside influences pulling us away from where we need to be. Such kindnesses mean we have to give energy, time, thought to the needs of the helper – to be gracious and grateful; not to be awkward, or embarrassing; making sure the other person is not burdened by our pain, etc. These considerations draw us from the time and opportunity just to feel what we feel without the need to explain ourselves. We want company – we don't want company; getting the balance is a tricky business, because, of course, the company we really want is denied us permanently and we are striving at all sorts of levels to come to grips with that immutable fact.

The people who love us may be grieving, too and they are concerned for us so there is a lot going on; caring, not wanting to get in the way, wanting to do and say the right things as well as having their own ideas about the process, and their own pain. Mainly, of course, they want the best for us even if neither they nor we can fully intuit what that means. All in all it is a very difficult time and we cannot help being aware of the different needs and desires of the other people involved. It is easy to find oneself on overload from all this excess of emotion, which is why we need to retire to our hermitage for a time.

The central idea of hermitage comes from the earliest centuries of Christianity when women and men chose to live in seclusion in the desert as a way of penance, to attain to a kind of martyrdom of the spirit when persecution for the faith ceased to be the guaranteed route to heaven. People opted for this way of life so that they could be free from the outside influences which seduced them from their highest desire, to come as close to the Divine as they could on this side of the grave. For these people, life in this world was merely a training ground for the life which was to come; death was not quite as tragic as it is 'in the world'.

On the one hand, in the ancient world, life expectancy was shorter than it is today and so people were more accustomed to the brevity of life. On the other hand, those people who chose the eremitic life had gladly given up human love for devotion to the Divine. The people they loved who had gone before were celebrated and rejoiced over as they had 'entered into the joy of their Lord'. They had gone to where the hermit was earnestly preparing for, by quiet contemplation. Free from distraction and worldly cares she was better able to concentrate on that which endures; meditating on the eternal and letting the rest of the world go by.

We may not share the world view of the ancients, but the idea of seclusion remains valuable for us, however busy our usual life may be. Sometimes we too need to let the rest of the world go by because we need the time to process, to remember and to allow our innermost being to begin the process of restoration. At the end of the book there is note on the background to the concept of 'hermit' for those who like to delve more deeply into symbolism.

THE SPACE BETWEEN

The space that separates us
and the space that connects us
is the same space.

Unknown

One universal fact which is now virtually undisputed is that everything in the universe is connected. This reality is now agreed upon by scientists of all persuasions; people who have undergone Near Death Experiences and mystics of all times and faiths. All is One. For the scientists, as one reads or listens, this oneness is now a provable fact; that is, provable to the rigorous standards of scientific research. For the N.D.E'ers and by many recorded words of mystics, it is an experiential reality. This reality is truly the point where science and spirituality meet (whatever the individual religious beliefs or lack thereof).

True knowledge of the Oneness is usually considered to approach the pinnacle of human experience. To have the perception, even for a brief moment, of this Oneness of all things is understood to be a point of transformation, never to be forgotten, that changes the way one perceives the world and one's own place in it; life and, importantly, death.

In the ordinary day to day life of most of us this is an experience never to be realised and so we find it both wonderful and bewildering to contemplate. We can, of course, accept the evidence of others and the arguments from common sense and believe in the truth that all is One, even without a personal mystical experience. To consider that belief, as we think about our loved ones, allows us to imagine at least that the space between our self and the ones that we can no longer see is not an empty space.

Because we can no longer see or touch the physical reality of our dear ones it can seem as though there is a vast space separating us from them. If we can allow ourselves to believe in a universe where everything is connected and nothing is lost then the space between us becomes the means of our connection as well as our separation. And we can speak into it, to accuse, to storm, to affirm, to pour out the variety of words and emotions that betray our confusion and our hurt.

In the silence that follows, if we stay put and listen, a new thought may emerge or a reassurance come in some other way. This silence, too, is an act of trust and of consolation if we will allow it.

THE RITUALS
– PUBLIC AND PRIVATE

There would be a funeral: black umbrellas, dripping
yews, muted voices, pious platitudes; then the
interested audience of old friends watching the
new creature emerge from its crepe chrysalis and
deciding whether it was admissible or not.

From *The Spy's Wife by Reginald Hill*

Funerals are often quite odd events these days.

Since the beginning of history, humans have buried their dead
with rituals of some sort. Indeed it is a theory among
anthropologists that one can mark the transition to 'modern man'
by the evidence of burial rites, and, of course, burial rites point to
religious beliefs of some sort.

Today we are in a curious situation in that a great many people do
not look for or want a religious context for funerals. Sometimes
we have a religious service, without any real devotion because 'that
is how it is done', but it is not too comfortable for many of the
congregation. The bible readings may be obscure, and talk about
resurrection and St. Paul's words about 'exchanging this body' etc.

can seem utterly weird, far outside the language and ideas we easily understand. For people of faith a full-on religious Service can be a wonderful means of dedication and hope, with the feeling that they have truly given over their loved one into the hands of a loving God.

In some ways these are the lucky ones, they are embedded in an age old form which, even by virtue of its continuity and solemnity, brings consolation and peace. For the rest it is hard to find a funeral service which is meaningful and reverent, comprehensible yet elevated, one that speaks to the hearts and minds of the people present. Often it develops into one or many narratives of the person's life story, a practice that probably belongs more comfortably to the Wake than the chapel, as it can be a torture for the bereaved, as well as the congregation, to have to sit through long story-telling in that place.

Funerals are for those who are left behind, to honour, do justice to or celebrate the departed; they may also be 'for God' if there is belief that the soul of the departed is being 'given into 'His' care', but mostly they are for the consolation and comfort of the bereaved. If we are the bereaved we have to get through it somehow, probably feeling more embarrassment overlaying the impossible sorrow than being comforted by the proceedings. On the other hand, not to have a funeral of any sort is difficult. Whatever else the funeral does, it gives a sense of finality to the earthly life we have shared with the person who has died. The time between the death and the funeral is weird; it is like living in some kind of vacuum, so the funeral is a necessary closure after which, in spite of the pain, life goes on. However oddly or inadequately we do it, we need rituals to mark the Big Moments in our lives.

We get through the funeral and aftermath as best we can, with whatever dignity we feel we can muster, but perhaps the more important and meaningful rituals are the private ones. The performance, quietly, deliberately and alone, of rituals that mark the passing of a loved one can be a very personal form of consolation.

In the old style of observance special prayers were said on the day of burial, on the third, seventh and thirtieth days after the death and on the anniversary, which was known as 'the year's mind'. This might be a useful framework but, privately, we would probably want something a bit more immediate and intimate, at least in the beginning. Candles, photographs, flowers, favourite music and books can all form part of our rituals, and silence, always some silence. Regularly to sit quietly, thoughtful and still is perhaps the best ritual of all, recalling the loved one and remembering that silence is the language of eternity. If we wish to have any sense of a continuing relationship we must adjust to the fact that silence is the means by which it can happen.

Having a project can help enormously: making something, it might be assembling a photo album of the high spots and meaningful events of your relationship or a video or other form of recording. Photographs are great. We seem to have less of them now, in hard copy, but to festoon the house with photos of happy events from the past is a great tribute to the life you have enjoyed. Of course, electronically you can have a series of photos constantly revolving which isn't quite the same as having pictures all over the house.

One of the most beautiful projects I have seen was made by a woman when her grown up son died, leaving a young son of his own. For her grandson, Margaret made a wonderful quilt. She had enlarged photos of the boy and his dad printed onto fabric which she then sewed into the quilt. Both sides were adorned and each background was fabric in the colours of their favourite football teams. What a labour of love! It was all for the boy but I am sure that the work kept Margaret focused on the creation which allowed her own grief just to be.

Writing is another special ritual to focus the mind. For example, you might write the story of the years you have spent together. This could one day be a real treasure for the next generation. Keeping a diary is one project that need never end. Every night you can write a few words about the day and about your feelings, addressed, not to yourself, but to the one with whom you would love to be reviewing the day. This can be a special comfort and it has the further great advantage that as time goes on you can read back and chart how you have changed and grown as the months/ years have passed. Diaries have the further benefit of being a record of memory. It is amazing how we can have insights and illuminations and as the days go by we forget what we thought unforgettable at the time. Reading these back, even years later, can be a revelation.

One of the surprising patterns that can emerge as time passes is that the recapitulation of the grief is more intense in the days leading up to a significant anniversary. This may not be only at the year's mind but birthdays, wedding anniversaries etc. The dawning of the actual day brings relief. I do not know why this should be but many people seem to find it so. A good idea is to plan in advance for the day; being left at a loose end can be uncomfortable. In some families a new ritual is devised for these days which becomes a family tradition when there is increasingly celebration of life, not only of the departed but of the family itself – a time for gratitude and appreciation.

Different cultures have their own ways of ritualising and marking the passing of a loved one. In one extreme there was the practice of sati which, thankfully, is no longer observed, though some people want to give vent to the wailing and moaning that is its natural accompaniment. Wearing black for a full year after the death of one's husband was once normal practice, sometimes even wearing it for the rest of one's life. Going into society within a year of his death was considered quite unseemly in a widow. A black band used to be a familiar sight on the arm of a man who was grieving, and can still be seen in the sporting arena to mark the death of a team mate or other significant person to the particular sport. People used to lower the blinds in the front room throughout the day to indicate a house was in mourning and flags are lowered to half-mast for the really famous. These are the sort of external reference points that honoured the state of bereavement.

We do not go in for these visible signs so much but that is no reason why we should short-change ourselves and 'press on regardless' when wailing and moaning is what we really want to do. Our own personal rituals can give us the space and time to process our emotions and allow us to feel that we are honouring ourselves and the one we still love though he or she is no longer present to us.

If prayer is a normal part of your life you will, of course engage with the practice according to your own inclination. Some people prefer to use words like 'Mindfulness' in order to create a distance from the formal practice that seems to be the property of Christians. Lovingly thinking of another, sending thoughts of compassion, pondering the reality of someone else's life, holding them in our hearts, these can all be understood as prayer for others.

There is one practice that is pertinent here and, for some, can bring relief and serenity, a form which rests in our common humanity rather than a religious code. Maybe the practice has a name, I do not know of one but this is a suggested form:

In times of pain, discomfort or distress you take some time to be quiet; you just give in, simply accepting and surrendering to the reality of whatever you are feeling. This acceptance focuses the mind and then after a time one shifts the attention to the heart and imagines it glowing, very bright, and you see the light of it reaching out to other people, in any part of the world, who are suffering in a similar way to you, whose loss and deprivation may well be more traumatic than your own. And you hold this focus for as long as feels right; you can come back to it, or vary it as often as you like. The practice has a way of making intuitive sense and calming something deep within; it does not need to be analysed, proved or justified. If it works for you that is all that matters.

THE NEED TO MATTER

There is a particular feeling which comes in different shapes for different people, but its roots lie in the need to matter. This is especially relevant to people who have lost a partner, whether one has lost the beloved through death or through betrayal. Perhaps it is also similar for some mothers whose children have left home. We are bound to the loved one as s/he is bound to us; we have the sense that someone else needs us, loves us, enjoys us, belongs to us – what are the words? I am trying to convey that sense of exclusivity – marriage as a secret society with a membership of two. In a loving partnership there is a mutual belonging, a uniqueness that is exclusive. No matter how many children we might have, friends or relations all of whom we love, there is, in the partnership, something that goes beyond all the other loves; is in a different category.

In that primary relationship we know that we matter in a very precise, particular and singular way. It may not always be expressed lovingly, indeed the very strength of it is expressed in the casual, the careless and occasionally the horrid, because the bond is so deeply embedded we do not have to be careful – perhaps we should be, but human nature being what it is, with those we are closest to we can afford sometimes to be off-hand.

At the loss of the loving one we are left not knowing if we matter anymore – we certainly do not matter in that very special way. Our friends and family all have their own lives to lead but this was our life – we had our own life to lead, our own particular cosy compartment – and now it does not exist and we cannot compensate by trying to barge in or sidle into the relationships of others.

We do not matter anymore as mattering is manifested by that primary relationship. We have to find other ways to salve our lost-ness. Many people do that by finding another partner, which is wonderful. But in the meantime, if a new partner does not come along, or if we are not interested in another lover, we have to embrace the truth and reality of what we feel and not pretend to ourselves that things are any different from what they are, no matter how much we may prevaricate for others,. We are not important as we once were, that is a big blow to the self, especially if the relationship was the most important thing in our life. There is a loss of identity; if I am no longer half of a couple who am I?

This is a very uncomfortable reality to live in, but it is better to acknowledge things to be what they are than to make the mistakes and create the problems that come from disguising this truth to ourselves. A worse state we can create is to feel these uncomfortable feelings and blame ourselves, "I shouldn't feel this way". Remember, whatever you feel is merely a fact. The feeling is neutral, it is neither 'good' nor 'bad'; it is simply what it is. What we do with it, how we manage it, that is where the judgement comes in, we can make things worse for ourselves by blame and shame or we can respect ourselves, honour our emotions and contain them. This is the process that brings us to a new state of awareness, leads us to a better self-understanding and prepares the way forward into the next stage of life.

We go forward into the next stage as an independent person, capable, self-reliant, and self-responsible. We make decisions for ourselves, usually good, sometimes disastrous, but they are ours, founded on what we believe is right for us at the time. It can be quite refreshing to discover what it is like to make decisions that do not have to be conditioned by someone else's needs, likes and dislikes.

Of course there are days of loneliness; not having that special someone there to share a joke or say "there, there" when we feel low. This is just horrid. It seems that such days do not go away, but we get to handle them better, by acceptance. All the gloom, the sadness, loneliness and drear do not amount to a sickness; they are the appropriate responses to grief. If we treat them as sickness we may be recommended on to the slippery slope of drug therapy which will numb the pain, but is likely to numb other feelings as well and to create a different brain state, subverting the natural process of grieving. This can prevent us coming through to the new sense of self and finding that independent, self-reliant person who has a new life to lead.

When we live in a relationship where we know that we matter it feels good, we are secure and our reliance can be located in the relationship or in the partner. This means that, to some degree, we project our security onto another and make them responsible for us. The level of security may not be obvious, it is not necessarily financial or material security but emotional, perhaps even spiritual. We all, to some extent, expect our partners to hold for us what as independent people we would care for for ourselves. For example, if one has a deep fear of abandonment one may find, within the partnership, the band-aid for that fear. The partner is security against being abandoned and, therefore, becomes responsible for one's emotional safety. This is a heavy burden, which is of course off-set by the equivalent bits the partner likewise projects.

This mutual projection is an unspoken deal that is struck, unconsciously, when we fall in love, or form any deep relationship. Some people would say this is the process of falling in love, we find just the right person to complement, hold or otherwise supply what we are unconsciously seeking in order to feel complete. The extent to which one does not own and carry for oneself the fear of abandonment is the extent to which one has not grown-up to be an adult in one's own right. Clearly, the departure of a beloved partner exposes us to the anxiety of managing those things which, maybe for years, we have not had to think about because our safety was guaranteed, held in our joint hermetic vessel.

Knowing that we matter fits into this pattern. I am sure that we will always want to enjoy mattering to someone, but grief can strip us of the need and the dependence on finding our worth in the eyes of a partner. Ultimately we must discover that we matter because we are, not because someone outside of us loves us. This, of course, is one of the great benefits of much religion, and I am not knocking it. To know beyond any shadow of doubt that one is loved by God can off-set any amount of agony and indecision. Then one can say, "I matter because I matter to God, I have great worth because God loves me." What a great and wonderful thing that is, to be sure of divine love! The real thing is, for a Christian, the true and total answer to the question of mattering. For those who do not find their consolation in God the road to the Self, however one travels it, can be rocky but, however tough, is ultimately vastly rewarding.

SPEAK NO ILL

He's in Arthur's bosom, if ever a man went to
Arthur's bosom

Henry V 1:3

Arthur's bosom is just one of the many names that has gone down
in history to define the place the departed go to when they are 'in
bliss'. This particular term comes from Shakespeare's *Henry V* and
it tells us where Falstaff's friends believe him to be, his having just
died. But they knew, better than most, what a thorough-going rogue
he was. He was a cheat, a thief, a womaniser, a liar, a drunkard; the
list goes on and on and yet for some reason he has the reputation of
being one of the best loved characters in the whole canon.

What was it about Falstaff that made his friends regret his passing
and believe him to have gone straight to heaven? If we find the
answer to that we might find the answer to our own attitudes
to the character of our departed loved ones. We have a way of
remembering and speaking of the attractive characteristics of the
departed and, if we mention their less agreeable parts, we do so
with gentle humour making them sound like a kind of virtue.
There is something here bigger than the courtesy of *de mortuis,*
the custom not to speak ill of the dead.

Mistress Quickly, who nursed Falstaff in his last hours, had many good reasons to speak ill of him and yet she grieves and believes in his translation to bliss. I want to try to explore what this means. It is as though when we love someone there is the essence of the person and there is what would be called 'the accidents'. The essence is who they essentially are, beyond the hardships, quirks, and disabilities, whether of mind or body which are the 'accidents' of a life. It is as though in loving someone we have access to this self, however much they may cloud it, deny it or live by brutalising it. In a way it is a bit like women who are abused by their husbands, who will stay with them no matter what. The women will often say, "He does love me really." And that is probably the truth. There is something about being bonded to a person that does just that – binds us.

We are bound in the unconscious and though we may be well aware of the shortcomings, irritations or even plain nastiness of someone we love, at their death it is that enduring self, that Real Self that came in as a baby and got terribly or mildly distorted by the exigencies of life that we remember and of whom we speak. This is fair enough, for the dross gets left behind with the body, the essential self is indestructible and eternal. For our purpose then it is not true that: *The evil that men do lives after them, the good is oft inter'ed with their bones.*

We may go through life from birth to death without any recognition or owning of that essential or Real Self. We may be married to someone for fifty years and the topic never be raised. The silence does not negate the truth that, despite all appearances; all the negligence, thoughtlessness, selfishness and want of kindness we know that beneath, behind and under all this painful stuff is the true person that we have always loved. At death that reality is what endures; it is what we remember and what we want to talk about and to celebrate.

> Life seems more sweet that thou didst live,
> And men more true that thou wert one;
> Nothing is lost that thou didst give,
> Nothing destroyed that thou hast done.

Anne Brontë

While all this may be true, there are situations when there is distress that is not easily laid aside to concentrate only on the enduring reality. But to go on through life with resentment can never be a good thing for the hurt souls left behind. Making an act of intention at the funeral can help us to focus and see that there is more to be done, sometime.

A good thing about planning funerals these days is that we are not confined to a set form so can makes inclusions etc. that are appropriate for our situation. We might include in the prayers something along these lines, which can of course be filled out as the situation deserves:

> During her/his life there have been
> disappointments, misunderstandings and hurt; at
> this time we release and let go of all the pain and
> we pray that the pain and disappointment we have
> caused may equally be forgiven.

FRIENDS AND RELATIONS

A good friend is my nearest relation

Thomas Fuller (1661)

Much of this book has been particularly addressed to grieving for our nearest and dearest. I have approached, only obliquely, through some of the poetry, the death of a child, which is the most unfathomable of human loss. Allowing this omission, the writing does have relevance to bereavement of anyone we have loved. Just for a moment I want to talk about the grief we can feel at the death of a friend.

As a friend we are in a different situation to family. We may not even be known to the family and yet we can be pierced with a grief as profound as ever we feel for a relation, and in many cases more so. We may know more truly about the likes and dislikes of the departed; what would or would not be appropriate rituals, according to their way of seeing the world and yet, as we are not family our views are usually not sought and we may have no say in the form of the funeral. At one level that seems normal, but in reality long-standing friends often do know us better than our family does.

Even if we are on friendly terms with the family our grieving is circumscribed by a need not to barge in, be intrusive or upstage the 'real mourners'. We often find our role is chief comforter, one who takes over practical tasks and this we gladly do. It is good to have a role, something to do, but there is still the grief which does not have the recognised outlet of those with a family connection. We may be feeling the loss more acutely than anyone in the family, but have to keep it to ourselves.

There is such an agenda about family grief that we can even question ourselves and contort the reality of our pain with thoughts like "Well it isn't as though I am one of the family" implying that the connection of blood somehow guarantees a greater right to a more significant grief. This is not so. The ties of friendship can be very strong, as we all know; in consequence, the depth of grief will reflect the depth of love in the friendship. Here is no conventional response born of situation or proximity. This is, some might say, the truest grief because it is born only of love, with no shoulds or oughts about it.

> A friend may well be reckoned a Masterpiece of Nature
>
> *R.W.Emerson (1882)*

> How often are we to die before we go quite off this stage? In every friend we lose a part of ourselves.
>
> *Alexander Pope (1744)*

A NOTE OFF KEY

Time, the clever thief
Taking all we have but grief

Alan Jenkins

It is a fact that we do not always feel as we think we should
when someone dies. This is particularly disconcerting when the
person is a relative, even a parent or sibling. If we are related by
blood there is a kind of mythology that says we must feel strong
grief and pain, if we don't we may be assured it will 'come later', that
if we don't let ourselves grieve now it will be worse when it hits us.
But sometimes it doesn't, it may not ever 'hit us' and we might feel
like some kind of freak or callous monster not to grieve at the death
of someone so close.

One way of dealing with this odd situation is, of course, to fake it,
in other words to go through the motions of grief for form's sake.
This may sound callous and dishonest, but at a death there is so
much going on, so much emotion, anxiety etc. from all the people
involved that keeping our head down while we process what is
going on for us can be easier, not only for ourselves, and it can save
us from the need to deal with awkward questions or responses.

Most people, at the time of a death, and especially during the days before the final leave-taking of the funeral, are struggling to come across as their normal selves. They are not their normal selves, of course, but the struggle is not only to appear to be okay but to hold our self together by clinging to the forms and customary ways of being. In all of this, lots of people behave quite oddly. If we take such oddity as, in its own way normal, we could avoid some of the extra pain that goes on at this time.

Funerals are not only times of straight, clear grief. Sorrow can come mixed up with darker, even more uncomfortable feelings. Where there is family, community involvement, indeed, ordinary human life there is going to be grimness, bad memories and ill-feeling around as well as the real sadness and grief. It may not be expressed, but there it is and we keep it under wraps for the ceremony. Sometimes there is a lot of feeling around that would be inappropriate to mention. At the funeral we remember the best of the person, and that is how it should be. But funerals and weddings are renowned for bringing out the long-standing family baggage; this is not surprising as either event shakes up the family dynamic. The familiar is being reconstituted in a new form, and the process is rarely to everyone's liking.

If we are able to take seriously the profound rearrangement and reorientation that has to go on in the psyche of those close to the departed we may begin to understand why there is such disruption and often disharmony in the family. And why the skeletons come creeping or darting out of the cupboard.

Maybe there is stuff that has been resented for years and now there is no possibility of straightening it out. In spite of the lovely mythology that people on their death-beds reveal a deeper understanding and wish to be reconciled with those they have offended this rarely seems to be the case. On the whole people die as they live. Someone who has spent their life believing in their own probity and correctness is not likely at the last to see themselves as fallible and in need of forgiveness. This can leave a wake of regret, sadness or a confusion of emotions that mixes resentment with a sense of guilt. We may, now it is too late, feel that perhaps we should have tried harder, or not been so stubborn with the one who has died and gone beyond the reach of reconciliation. Or we may in fact hate them just as much as we did before, while not really being easy in our mind about that either.

These days one of the familiar causes of distress, dissension and pain is where there is more than one family involved, as when the deceased has been married more than once and there being children from each marriage. Some people are able to manage this situation with grace and charm, but often the death proves to be the solvent that releases the bitterness and resentment that has been bottled up for years. This is one time where the symbolism of money is most apparent. All the pent up hurt, feelings of rejection, abandonment and deprivation can come out in the squabbles over the estate. Of course these are issues in their own right, but the venom which can be expressed has more to do with the pains both historic and present than with the actual dollars and cents involved – however many of them there maybe.

What with the deficiencies on both sides that we know about but hesitate to mention and the turmoil that is going on outside of our awareness, it is not surprising that people behave oddly and that family patterns are disrupted. Tenderness, gentleness with ourselves and the other vulnerable people around us, if we can manage it, is the best way through. This starts with the recognition that this is an extraordinary time and that nothing is going to be normal for a while so do not expect too much of yourself or of anyone else. We all struggle and what we do not say is of more significance than what we do and what we know is so much less than what we do not know about other people's love, life, sadness or regrets.

These days, grief, as with almost everything else about the human condition, has been 'under the microscope' and can now be explained in highly scientific language. This is not very much help to the people who are grieving, except, maybe, to give a kind of validation (if such is needed) to the feelings, if we are tempted to get into "I shouldn't be going on like this" or "Why doesn't she get over it?" What the science boils down to is this, that when you have suffered a loss, your brain has a lot of processing to do to reorganise how it will now perceive the world without that particular person or persons. It has to recalibrate, and this takes longer the longer we have known someone.

When you are grieving, take time to rest, accept, and allow the process to happen. It may be difficult, but your head will return to normal in time. And remember, other people are coping in their own ways and their time frame may be quite different to your own, that does not matter; stay with what is real for you.

THE CHRISTIAN STORY

The basic message of Christianity, however anyone may argue otherwise, is that we should know that we are utterly loved by God and that nothing can separate us from God's love. That is the heart and soul of Christianity and it was the core of St. Paul's message:

> For I am convinced that neither death nor life, nor
> angels, nor rulers, nor things present, nor things
> to come, nor powers, nor height, nor depth nor
> anything else in all creation will be able to separate
> us from the love of God in Christ Jesus

Romans 8:38

St. Paul's stress on the love of God in time gave way to a greater stress on sin, and God's judgement. As with much church teaching, historically, the obsession with sin blurred everything else so that God's judgement overshadowed His love. His mercy, which once meant His overarching care, came to have a more forensic interpretation. This was a great way of controlling the populace in the olden days but today it is an anachronism that burdens the Christian message.

There is a famous story from the Celtic Church of the seventh century about a queen called Ethelburga. She won her husband and his whole realm from paganism to Christianity because that faith, she believed, had something trustworthy to say about the life to come. This is Bede's account of the event:

> When we compare the present life of man with that time of which we have no knowledge, it seems to me like the swift flight of a lone sparrow through the banqueting hall where you sit in the winter months to dine with your thanes and counsellors. Inside there is a comforting fire to warm the room; outside the wintry storms of snow and rain are raging. This sparrow flies swiftly in through one door of the hall, and out through another. While he is inside, he is safe from the winter storms; but after a few moments of comfort, he vanishes from sight into the darkness from whence he came. Similarly man appears on earth for a little while, but we know nothing of what went before this life, and what follows. Therefore, if this new teaching can reveal any more certain knowledge, it seems only right that we should follow it.

The ancient Celtic Church held close to the spiritual realities and was not hampered by seventeen hundred years of organisational development and a scientific revolution. The contemporary church does not give out the kind of whole-hearted certainty the ancients took for granted; generally it is reticent to speak of life after death.

The faith that fired off the Christian mission in the beginning was that Jesus, though dead, was alive and had appeared to His friends and disciples; the clearest possible statement that death was not the end and that where He was all could follow. The delineation between those who believed in Him and those who did not created the division between those who would join Him in Heaven and those who would go to 'the other place'.

We do not hold to that kind of pictorial or literal definition of place, neither do we generally make the hard and fast rulings about who is in and who is not. The historical relevance of that way of thinking is not applicable to the present time. Belief got stuck on the antique idea of a Day of Judgement, before which time all shall sleep. There is not a neat generally accepted definition among Christians about what this means. The creeds affirm that Jesus will come again 'to judge the living and the dead' so this is strongly embedded in the tradition. The belief seems to cast doubt on the possibility of ongoing consciousness or communication.

That the church is uncomfortable with manifestations of life beyond the grave is odd since the central tenet of the faith is the Resurrection of Christ. The New Testament has many things to say about the Hereafter, and we have heard some of them often at Christian Funeral Services, but for a very long time the church has been diffident about entering into discussion of the topic; to make any affirming statements or to listen attentively to people's experiences when they are out of what is considered to be the norm.

Because Church teaching is so bound into the forms and definitions of the past it is difficult to express belief in the Life Hereafter in terms that are both true to tradition and to the contemporary understanding of the Universe. The topic, therefore, tends to end up in the proverbial 'too hard' basket. When we are bereaved, the 'too hard' basket feels a bit like home and where we may be looking for some guide-lines, some consolation, something that helps us make a bit of sense of all that feels beyond sense or reason.

Of course there are many splendid writings from Christians who do want to help us make sense of the great mystery; who offer wonderful words of consolation and encouragement that can support us in difficult times. Here are some favourite pieces from a French Abbé of the late nineteenth century who had a glorious grip on reality:

> If you are truly at peace with God, have no shadow of fear of death. Death only appears painful to those on earth. The departed do not think thus. In the wonderful surprise of a new life, they are happier than when they first realised life on earth.

> We should look upon the dead as happy living beings and rejoice wholeheartedly in their good fortune. We should realise that we are in constant intercourse with them, because they are elect souls and because our world is only separated from theirs by a veil. We should realise that this veil does not separate us from God, nor from the society of those who are with God.

> Human life is by no means limited to its short passage through this world. Death is only an illusion which hides from us the continuing development of

life. And, moreover, we are generally dead in many respects before the actual moment which completes our transformation. Interior changes gradually make us realize that, in spite of all our vicissitudes, we are indeed immortal, with a life, an endless activity, which death does not cut short: far from it.

Whatever time therefore, we may have lost in this world through circumstances which have checked our activity, is a small matter compared to the life without end which dwells in us and which will easily catch us up later on.

···

Life limited by death? Nonsense! That is a great mistake. Death hardly counts; it is a mere appearance; we already have eternal life and that reflection should give us great tranquillity, as those who feel themselves to be eternal.

Abbé de Tourville (1903)

This following piece was written by an Anglican bishop, the Rt. Rev. Stephen Verney (2001) after the death of his wife:

After her death there was that numbness which comes to everyone after the shock of bereavement. Then, after a couple of days, the conviction that I must remember her and help her on her way, but at the same time that I must not cling to her and hold her back. Over the following days and weeks I felt an increasing awareness of her presence, a deep communion of spirit with spirit in a new found freedom. Now there were no marriage bonds, no compulsive interaction, no pretence, but a new possibility of love and co-operation. It was as though death had done for us what we could only partly achieve in this life. It has torn us apart at great cost, broken our dependence upon each other, made us independent, and opened up the possibility of interdependence. But I should not say death had done it –the divine love was doing it through death, and through resurrection.

Now I was being grasped by a truth which formerly I was trying to grasp – a belief in the resurrection of the dead and the life of the age to come. This truth was not dependent on extra-sensory perception, though many people have told me how quite un-hysterically and unexpectedly they have seen again those whom they had loved and lost. A number of coincidences occurred which were utterly astonishing and convincing and brought message of love – but these are only convincing to the people to whom they happen, and in any case they are only peripheral signs. The central awareness was that in spite of all our sin (and I use the word in its exact sense of our failure to be ourselves, to keep covenant with each other, and to have faith) my true self and her true self were held together by the divine love, as the two halves of a cracked piece of wood are held together by an unbreakable rivet of steel

Stephen Verney Into the New Age

Another means of strength and consolation within the Christian church is the tradition of formal prayers. There are some beautiful prayers, both ancient and modern which can support and encourage faith in the love of God and the well-being of the departed. I have included a few here from various traditions within the church, but I have chosen not to include any that dwell on judgement and sin.

> Grant, O Lord, to all who are bereaved, the spirit of faith and courage, that they may have the strength to meet the days to come with steadfastness and patience; not sorrowing as those without hope but in thankful remembrance of thy great goodness in past years and in the sure expectation of a joyful reunion in the heavenly places; and this we ask in the name of Jesus Christ our Lord.

> Almighty God, Father of all mercies and giver of all comfort;
> Deal graciously, we pray, with those who mourn, that, casting all their cares on you they may know the consolation of your love;
> through Jesus Christ our Lord.

> Heavenly Father,
> In your Son Jesus Christ you have given us a true faith and a sure hope. Help us to live as those who believe in the communion of saints, the forgiveness of sins, and the resurrection to eternal life through your Son Jesus Christ our Lord.

Eternal Father, God of all consolation, in your unending love and mercy for us you turn the darkness of death into the dawn of new life. Be our refuge and strength in sorrow.

As your Son, our Lord Jesus Christ, by dying for us conquered death and by rising again restored us to life, so may we go forward in faith to meet him and after our life on earth be united with our dear brothers and sisters in Christ where every tear will be wiped away. We ask this through Jesus Christ our Lord.

Have compassion, O Lord, upon all who are mourning for those dear to them, and upon all who are lonely and desolate. Be thou their comforter and friend; give them such earthly help and consolation as thou seest best for them; and grant them a fuller knowledge and realisation of thy love; for thy holy name's sake.

Grant, O Lord, that keeping in glad remembrance those who have gone before, who have stood by us and helped us, who have cheered us by their sympathy and strengthened us by their example, we may seize every opportunity of life and rejoice in the promise of a glorious resurrection with them: through Jesus Christ our Lord.

Support us, O Lord, all the day long of this
troublesome life
Until the shades lengthen, the evening comes, the
busy world is hushed, the fever of life is over and our
work done.
Then Lord in thy mercy,
Grant us a safe lodging
A holy rest and peace at the last:
Through Christ our Lord.

Poetry has, as far back as we can go, been a means of making sense of life and especially death for both the writer and the reader. Many, many poets, ancient and modern, have exorcised their grief by turning it to verse. Some have written out of a deep faith and found their peace in the Gospel promises; some have been consoled by the sense of abiding presence, some have found no consolation other than in the writing. In the next chapter I have collected an array of works suited to various moods and states of grief in the hope that some days you will find words to meet you; capture what you are feeling or remind you that others have trod this path before you and understand the pain, though you may not always understand their way of putting it. No matter. You do not have to understand all that you read; the words work at intuitive levels especially if you don't work too hard and just allow familiarity to do it for you.

THE POETRY OF GRIEF

Sometimes we do not want to read comforting, bracing or consoling words. The only glimmer of consolation may be in knowing that other people have suffered in ways similar to ourselves. No suffering is just the same as mine, yet reading of another's pain may be the only connection I can make. Here is a hand reaching out to me from the depth of a comparable misery; it is the only hand I can take today. Probably we don't want to read anything about which we need to think, either. Emotions are raw, primitive; a few words here and there are likely to help the most. In this chapter I have collected some pieces written by people whose business was with words and so, even expressing sorrow, they can capture what we feel when grief strikes us to the bone but we have no words of our own to say truly what we feel.

Nothing is constant, not even the pain, it changes, morphs into a new mode, then reverses again to the familiar ache as our resolutions to think clearly and be grateful for what we once had descends again to the abyss of loss. And so we go on, sometimes only just, with little clarity and, daily, with the desire to let go and join the beloved: truly 'in the midst of life we are in death'. One perception that returns again and again is the sense that it has only just happened – it was only yesterday that he/she died. As Albert

Einstein is reputed to have said, "The distinction between past, present and future is only an illusion, however persistent." In our grief, this scientific assertion becomes experienced reality.

> I dreamt of you again last night. And when I woke
> up it was as if you had died afresh. Every day I find
> it harder to bear. For what point is there in life
> now? ... I look at our favourites, I try to read them,
> but without you they give me no pleasure. I only
> remember the evenings when you read them aloud
> to me and then I cry.

This is from the diary of the artist Dora Carrington (1932) grieving for her lost lover, Lytton Strachey. Carrington lasted less than three months after Strachey's death. Whether in the past or the present day this experience is the same; when the one we love has gone we go through times of feeling that there is just no point to life. Why bother?

> He first deceased; she for a little tried
> To live without him; lik'd it not and died.
>
> *Sir Henry Woton (1639)*

When we feel this way the 'time is a great healer' story does not work either. As the writer Ivy Crompton-Burnett says "Time has too much credit..... it is not a great healer. It is an indifferent and perfunctory one. Sometimes it does not heal at all. And sometimes when it seems to no healing has been necessary."

> Time does not bring relief; you all have lied
> Who told me time would ease the pain
> I miss him in the weeping of the rain;
> I want him at the shrinking of the tide.

> *Edna St. Vincent Millay (1950)*

Countless times we turn to speak as we used to, to share a joke or recount the day's happenings. We come home and there is no-one to tell about the funny thing that happened, or to whinge to about the speeding fine or a thousand incidental things we used not to think twice about sharing and then forgetting. For Wordsworth it was the joyous things he couldn't share that brought this home to him:

Surprised By Joy

> Surprised by joy — impatient as the Wind
> I turned to share the transport — Oh! with whom
> But Thee, long buried in the silent Tomb,
> That spot which no vicissitude can find?
> Love, faithful love recalled thee to my mind —
> But how could I forget thee? — Through what
> power, Even for the least division of an hour,
> Have I been so beguiled as to be blind

To my most grievous loss? — That thought's return
Was the worst pang that sorrow ever bore,
Save one, one only, when I stood forlorn,
Knowing my heart's best treasure was no more;
That neither present time, nor years unborn
Could to my sight that heavenly face restore.

William Wordsworth (1850)

Grief

I cannot tell you any more
when the jonquils show
their scented heads under
that gnarled tree.
I cannot tell you
when the seeds thrust green
through this now black earth.

And the twice turned twice
furrowed soil trenched over,
fallow farrowed soil
lies bare.

I found that hoe you looked for
everywhere
and turned to tell you,
but your bent back

over some wayward plant
or small discovered toad, gently
held in your hands, was
not there.

Mary Dilworth

And we are all inclined to do simple acts that would seem daft at
any other time. Now they make complete sense to us and absorb the
focus of our full attention; like standing outside a house in the wee,
small hours, looking at windows behind which, once for us, life was
engaging. The stanzas that follow are from a poem by Alfred, Lord
Tennyson, written out of his misery at the death of a friend.

from *In Memoriam*

Dark house, by which once more I stand
Here in the long unlovely street,
Doors, where my heart was used to beat
So quickly, waiting for a hand,

A hand that can be clasp'd no more —
Behold me, for I cannot sleep,
And like a guilty thing I creep
At earliest morning to the door.

He is not here; but far away
The noise of life begins again,
And ghastly thro' the drizzling rain
On the bald street breaks the blank day.

Nevertheless, in spite of his overwhelming grief he could still say:

> I hold it true, what e'er befall;
> I feel it when I sorrow most;
> 'Tis better to have loved and lost
> Than never to have loved at all.

Alfred, Lord Tennyson (1892)

C.S. Lewis claimed that "bereavement is a universal and integral part of our experience of love. It follows as marriage follows courtship and as autumn follows summer." Though this is undoubtedly true, it seems quite irrelevant when we are pining for the loved one who has gone. Here is a section of a much older poem, from the seventeenth century. Sometimes old, formal language works for us; the sonorous tones resonating with the depth and solemnity of our experience.

The Exequy

> Accept, thou shrine of my dead saint,
> Instead of dirges, this complaint;
> And for sweet flow'rs to crown thy hearse,
> From thy griev'd friend, whom thou might'st see
> Quite melted into tears for thee.
> Dear loss! since thy untimely fate
> My task hath been to meditate
> On thee, on thee; thou art the book,
> The library whereon I look,
> Though almost blind. For thee (lov'd clay)
> I languish out, not live, the day,

Using no other exercise
But what I practise with mine eyes;
By which wet glasses I find out

How lazily time creeps about
To one that mourns; this, only this,
My exercise and bus'ness is.
So I compute the weary hours
With sighs dissolved into showers.

Sleep on my love in thy cold bed
Never to be disquieted!
My last good-night! Thou wilt not wake
Till I thy fate shall overtake;

Till age, or grief, or sickness must
Marry my body to that dust
It so much loves, and fill the room
My heart keeps empty in thy tomb.
Stay for me there, I will not fail
To meet thee in that hollow vale.
And think not much of my delay;
I am already on the way,
And follow thee with all the speed
Desire can make, or sorrows breed.
Each minute is a short degree,
And ev'ry hour a step towards thee.
At night when I betake to rest,
Next morn I rise nearer my west
Of life, almost by eight hours' sail,
Than when sleep breath'd his drowsy gale.

Henry King (1669)

Perhaps (To R.A.L.)

Perhaps someday the sun will shine again,
And I shall see that still the skies are blue,
And feel once more I do not live in vain,
Although bereft of You.

Perhaps the golden meadows at my feet
Will make the sunny hours of spring seem gay,
And I shall find the white May-blossoms sweet,
Though You have passed away.

Perhaps the summer woods will shimmer bright,
And crimson roses once again be fair,
And autumn harvest fields a rich delight,
Although You are not there.

Perhaps some day I shall not shrink in pain
To see the passing of the dying year,
And listen to Christmas songs again,
Although You cannot hear.'

But though kind Time may many joys renew,
There is one greatest joy I shall not know
Again, because my heart for loss of You
Was broken, long ago.

Vera Brittain (1970)

Dirge Without Music

I am not resigned to the shutting away of loving hearts
                            in the hard ground.
So it is, and so it will be, for so it has been, time out of
                                                    mind;
Into the darkness they go, the wise and the lovely.
                                            Crowned
With lilies and with laurels they go; but I am not
                            resigned.

Lovers and thinkers into the ground with you
Be one with the dull indiscriminate dust.
A fragment of what you felt of what you knew,
A formula, a phrase remains, - but the best is lost.

The answers quick and keen, the honest look, the
                                    laughter, the love –
They are gone. They are gone to feed the roses.
                                    Elegant and curled
Is the blossom. Fragrant is the blossom. I know.
                                    But I do not approve
More precious was the light in your eyes than all the
                                            roses in the world

Down, down, down into the darkness of the grave
Gently they go, the beautiful, the tender, the kind;
Quietly they go, the intelligent, the witty, the brave.
I know. But I do not approve. And I am not resigned.

Edna St. Vincent Millay (1950)

Sometimes Even Now...

Sometimes even now I may
Steal a prisoner's holiday.
Slip, when all is worst, the bands
   Hurry back, and duck beneath
Time's old tyrannous groping hands
   Speed away with laughing breath
Back to all I'll ever know,
Back to you, a year ago

Truant there from Time and Pain,
What I had I find again:
Sunlight in the boughs above,
   Sunlight in your hair and dress,
The Hands too proud for all but Love,
   The Lips of utter kindliness,
The heart of bravery swift and clean
   Where the best was safe, I knew,
And laughter in the gold and green,
   And song, and friends, and ever you
With smiling and familiar eyes,
   You – but friendly: you – but true.

And Innocence accounted wise,
   And Faith, the fool, the pitiable.
Love so rare, one would swear
   All of earth forever well –
Careless lips and flying hair
   And little things I may not tell.

It does but double the heart-ache
When I wake, when I wake.

Rupert Brooke (1915)

Dying, you have left behind you the great sadness of
the Eternal in my life. You have painted my thought's
horizon with the sunset colours of your departure,
leaving a track of tears across the earth to love's
heaven. Clasped in your dear arms, life and death
united in me in a marriage bond.

I think I can see you watching there in the balcony
with your lamp lighted, where the end and the
beginning of all things meet. My world went once
through the doors that you opened – you holding
the cup of death to my lips, filling it with life from
your own.

Rabindanath Tagore (1941)

W.H. Auden knew the agony of grief and he also knew that the rest of
the world could go blithely on, ignoring the tragedy. It is bewildering
to find everything else is going on normally when we are in the midst
of woe and despair. In his *Musée des Beaux Arts* Auden captures that
weird sense that the world somehow ought to be reflecting our
sorrow, but, in fact, it goes on its merry way, regardless of our gloom.

His poem *Stop all the clocks*, won many people over to the value
of poetry in times of grief after seeing the film *Four Weddings
and a Funeral*. He conveys so well the feeling of hopelessness and
pointlessness that we feel. In language and imagery that is ordinary
he weaves a profound expression of bereavement.

Another modern poet whose works you might find consoling is Robert Graves. His *Wherever we may be* and *The Theme of Death* are lovely, and speak to us of the pain of loving. The Australian poet Judith Wright is so worth checking out, too. These poems, by twentieth century writers are not easy to reprint, but you can find them and many, many more on the net.

As poets write out of their sense of loss and their pain, they have words for us that we cannot find for ourselves. Sometimes we find ease from words poets have imagined as coming from the Beloved, beyond death, or in the remembrance of beautiful days now past; sometimes it is the misery that we feel will never end. There is also, like Hamlet, the profound wish for our own death to close the gap:

> O, that this too too solid flesh would melt,
> Thaw, and resolve itself into a dew!
> Or that the Everlasting had not fix'd
> His canon 'gainst self-slaughter! O God! God!
> How weary, stale, flat, and unprofitable,
> Seem to me all the uses of this world!
> Fie on't! Ah, fie! 'tis an unweeded garden,
> That grows to seed; things rank and gross in nature
> possess it merely.

from *The Burning of the Leaves*

Now is the time for stripping the spirit bare,
Time for the burning of days ended and done,
Idle solace of things that have gone before:
Rootless hopes and fruitless desire are there;
Let them go to the fire, with never a look behind
The world that was ours is a world that is ours
                                no more.

Lawrence Binyon (1943)

The Watch

I wakened on my hot, hard bed,
Upon the pillow lay my head;
Beneath the pillow I could hear
My little watch was ticking clear.

I thought the throbbing of it went
Like my continual discontent;
I thought it said in every tick:
I am so sick, so sick, so sick;
O Death, come quick, come quick, come quick,
Come quick, come quick, come quick, come quick.

Frances Cornford (1960)

from *The Wayfarers*

...Do you think there's a far border town,
  somewhere,
The desert's edge, last of the lands we know,
   Some gaunt eventual limit of our light,
In which I'll find you waiting; and we'll go
Together, hand in hand again, out there,
   Into the waste we know not, into the night?

Rupert Brooke (1915)

Liberty

The last light has gone out of the world, except
This moonlight lying on the grass like frost
Beyond the brink of the tall elm's shadow,
It is as if everything else had slept
Many an age, unforgotten and lost –
The men that were, the things done, long ago,
All I have thought; and but the moon and I
Live yet and here stand idle over a grave
Where all is buried. Both have liberty
To dream what we could do if we were free
To do something we had desired long,
The moon and I. There's none less free than who
Does nothing and has nothing else to do,
Being free only for what is not to his mind,
And nothing is to his mind. If every hour
Like this one passing that I have spent among
The wiser others when I have forgot
To wonder whether I was free or not,
Were piled before me, and not lost behind,
And I could take and carry them away

I should be rich; or if I had the power
To wipe out every one and not again
Regret, I should be rich to be so poor.
And yet I still am half in love with pain,
With what is imperfect, with both tears and mirth,
With things that have an end, with life and earth,
And this moon that leave me dark within the door.

Edward Thomas (1917)

Here are a couple of little quotes from Queen Elizabeth, the Queen Mother, who died in 2002. She lived fifty years after the death of her husband, and she always understood what grief was about.

> How small and selfish is death. But it bangs one about until one is senseless

> One will never feel the same again. I talk and laugh and listen, but......one's real self dies when one's husband dies and only a ghost remains. The only things that rouse me to anger are when people look at me in a penetrating way, and say "are you feeling BETTER.." If only they knew!

Too soon

Too soon, too soon comes Death to show
We love more deeply than we know.
The rain, that fell upon the height
Too gently to be called delight,
Within the dark vale reappears,
As a wild cataract of tears;
And love in life should strive to see
Sometimes what love in death would be.

Coventry Patmore (1896)

Afterthought

How simple is my burden every day
Now you have died, till I am dead,
The words, "Forgive me", that I could not say,
The words 'I am sorry', that you might have said.

Frances Cornford (1960)

Spell Against Sorrow

WHO will take away
Carry away sorrow,
Bear away grief?
Stream wash away

Float away sorrow,
Flow away, bear away
Wear away sorrow,
Carry away grief.

Mists hide away
Shroud my sorrow,
Cover the mountains,
Overcloud remembrance,
Hide away grief.

Earth take away
Make away sorrow,
Bury the lark's bones
Under the turf.
Bury my grief

Black crow tear away
Rend away sorrow,
Talon and beak
Pluck out the heart
And the nerves of pain,
Tear away grief.

Sun, take away
Melt away sorrow,
Dew lies grey
Rain hangs on the grass,
Sun dry tears.

Sleep take away
Make away sorrow,
Take away the time,
Fade away the place,
Carry me away

From the world of my sorrow.
Song sigh away
Breathe away sorrow,
Words tell away
Spell away sorrow,
Charm away grief.

Kathleen Raine (2003)

Remember

Remember me when I am gone away,
Gone far away into the silent land,
When you can no more hold me by the hand,
Nor I half turn to go yet turning stay.
Remember me when no more day by day
You tell me of our future that you plann'd:
Only remember me; you understand
It will be late to counsel then or pray.
Yet if you should forget me for a while
And afterwards remember, do not grieve:
For if the darkness and corruption leave
A vestige of the thoughts that once I had,
Better by far you should forget and smile
Than that you should remember and be sad.

Christina Rossetti (1894)

Sleeping at last

Sleeping at last, the trouble and tumult over,
Sleeping at last, the struggle and horror past,
Cold and white, out of sight of friend and of lover,
Sleeping at last.

No more a tired heart downcast or overcast,
No more pangs that wring or shifting fears that
                                          hover,
Sleeping at last in a dreamless sleep locked fast.

Fast asleep. Singing birds in their leafy cover
Cannot wake her, nor shake her the gusty blast.
Under the purple thyme and the purple clover
Sleeping at last.

Christina Rossetti

We have known treasure

We have known treasure fairer than a dream
Upon the hills of youth and it shall stay
Jewelled in the distance, untarnished and supreme.
For the dark tentacles of life's decay shall never
                                          shadow it
Nor overthrow its years like hours grown golden in
                                          the sun.
Its years lived full in the gathered light;
An amethyst across the sea of night.

For dawn and dusk we knew and caught our breath
With the exquisite 'maginings of spring;
Lived deep, talked lightly of this stranger, death

And love grown wistful with remembering
A half familiar tune we used to sing, these were ours.
Love's touch upon our hands, music and flowers;
Though in the faithless years they have no part
These are the endless things, the real of heart

Anon

Reflections on Friendship

They that live Beyond the World cannot be separated
                                                    by it
Death cannot kill what never dies
Nor can Spirits ever be divided that love and live in
the same Divine Principle; the Root and
Record of their Friendship.
If Absence be not Death, neither is their's.
Death is but a Crossing the World, as Friends do the
Seas. They live in one another still
For they must needs be present, that love and live in
                        that which is Omnipresent.
In this Divine Glass, they see Face to Face; and their
                        converse is Free as well as Pure.
This is the Comfort of Friends, that though they may
be said to Die, yet their Friendship and Society are in
the best Sense, ever present, because Immortal.

From *Some Fruits of Solitude by William Penn (1718)*

Fear No More

Fear no more the heat o' the sun,
Nor the furious winter's rages;
Thou thy worldly task hast done,
Home art gone, and ta'en thy wages:
Golden lads and girls all must,
As chimney sweepers come to dust.

Fear no more the frown o' the great,
Thou art past the tyrant's stroke;
Care no more to clothe and eat;
To thee the reed is as the oak;
The sceptre, learning, physic, must
All follow this, and come to dust.

Fear no more the lightning-flash,
Nor the all-dreaded thunder-stone;
Fear not slander, censure rash;
Thou hast finish'd joy and moan:
All lovers young, all lovers must
Consign to thee, and come to dust.

No exorciser harm thee!
Nor no witchcraft charm thee!
Ghost unlaid forbear thee!
Nothing ill come near thee!
Quiet consummation have;
And renowned be thy grave!

William Shakespeare (1616)

"Peace, peace he is not dead" these are the words we long to hear. Even though we know that our beloved is no longer here with us in the flesh we want to believe that death is truly not the end. Here are some writers who believe, beyond doubt, in Life and affirm, quite gloriously, what we all need to hear.

The following piece is a quote taken from the tape of a lecture given by The Most Rev. George Appleton, sometime Archbishop of Perth. He was a saintly man with a deep conviction of the Life Hereafter who spoke often of his experience of his wife after she left this world. His taped addresses to the Churches' Fellowship for Psychical and Spiritual Studies are in themselves quite poetic and deeply inspirational. This is one of his most beautiful quotes taken from the writings of the theologian Ladistlaus Boros (1981)

> Every genuine lover affirms: it is impossible for you not to be always with me. I myself, loving you as I do, would no longer exist if you no longer did, but I am alive and therefore so are you; even if you are far from me, even beyond the grave. I shall, perhaps, receive no sign of your presence but between us there need be no sign and no verification. Nothing that happens to us can destroy this eternity inherent in our love. I should be consenting to your destruction and my own, denying the very nature of our love and, to the extent that is in my power, I should be handing you over to eternal death if I did not affirm with all the force of my very existence as a person that you will live on after death, whatever the superficial evidence to the contrary.

from *Adonais*

XXXIX

Peace, peace! he is not dead, he doth not sleep -
He hath awakened from the dream of life -
'Tis we, who lost in stormy visions, keep
With phantoms an unprofitable strife,
And in mad trance, strike with our spirit's knife
Invulnerable nothings. - We decay
Like corpses in a charnel; fear and grief
Convulse us and consume us day by day,
And cold hopes swarm like worms within
our living clay

XL

He has outsoared the shadow of our night;
Envy and calumny and hate and pain,
And that unrest which men miscall delight,
Can touch him not and torture not again;
From the contagion of the world's slow stain
He is secure, and now can never mourn
A heart grown cold, a head grown grey in vain;
Nor, when the spirit's self has ceased to burn,
With sparkless ashes load an unlamented urn.

L111

Why linger, why turn back, why shrink, my Heart?
They hopes are gone before: from all things here
They have departed; thou shouldst now depart!
A light is passed from the revolving year,
And man, and woman; and what still is dear
Attracts to crush, repels to make thee wither.

The soft sky smiles, - the low wind whispers near:
'Tis Adonais calls! oh, hasten thither,
No more let Life divide what Death can join together.

P.B.Shelley.(1822)

If the birds are making lamentation, or the green
banks are moved by a little wind of summer, or you
can hear the waters making a stir by the shores that
are green and flowery.

   That is where I do be stretched out thinking of
love, writing my songs, and herself that heaven show
me though hidden in the earth I set my eyes on,
and hear the way that she feels my sighs and makes
answer to me.

   'Alas,' I hear her say, 'why are you using yourself up
before the time is come and pouring out a stream of
tears so sad and doleful.

   You'd do right to be glad rather, for in dying I won
days that have no ending, and when you saw me
shutting up my eyes I was opening them on the
light eternal.'

Petrarch (1374) (trans J.M. Synge)

from *Severed and Gone*

Life seems more sweet that thou didst live,
And men more true that thou wert one;
Nothing is lost that thou didst give,
Nothing destroyed that thou hast done.

Earth hath received thy earthly part;
Thy heavenly flame hath heavenward flown;
But both still live within my heart,
Still live, and not in mine alone.

Anne Brontë (1849)

Sonnet XLIII

How do I love thee? Let me count the ways.
I love thee to the depth and breadth and height
My soul can reach, when feeling out of sight
For the ends of Being and ideal Grace.
I love thee to the level of every day's
Most quiet need, by sun and candlelight.
I love thee freely, as men strive for Right;
I love thee purely, as they turn from Praise.
I love thee with the passion put to use
In my old griefs, and with my childhood's faith.
I love thee with a love I seemed to lose
With my lost saints, - I love thee with the breath,
Smiles, tears, of all my life! – and, if God choose,
I shall love thee better after death.

Elizabeth Barrett Browning (1861)

Death is nothing at all.

Death is nothing at all.
I have only slipped away to the next room.
I am I and you are you.
Whatever we were to each other,
That, we still are.
Call me by my old familiar name.
Speak to me in the easy way
which you always used.
Put no difference into your tone.
Wear no forced air of solemnity or sorrow.

Laugh as we always laughed
at the little jokes we enjoyed together.
Play, smile, think of me. Pray for me.
Let my name be ever the household word
that it always was.
Let it be spoken without effect.
Without the trace of a shadow on it.

Life means all that it ever meant.
It is the same that it ever was.
There is absolute unbroken continuity.
Why should I be out of mind
because I am out of sight?

I am but waiting for you.
For an interval.
Somewhere. Very near.
Just around the corner.
All is well.

Henry Scott Holland (1918)

They who are near to me

They who are near to me do not know that you are
nearer to me than they are.
They who speak to me do not know that my heart is
full with your unspoken words.
They who crowd in my path do not know that I am
walking alone with you.
They who love me do not know that their love brings
you to my heart.

Rabindranath Tagore (1941)

Come to me in my dreams

Come to me in my dreams, and then
By day I shall be well again!
For so the night will more than pay
The hopeless longing of the day.

Come, as thou cam'st a thousand times,
A messenger from radiant climes,
And smile on thy new world, and be
As kind to others as to me!

Or, as thou never cam'st in sooth,
Come now, and let me dream it truth,
And part my hair, and kiss my brow,
And say, My love why sufferest thou?

Come to me in my dreams, and then
By day I shall be well again!
For so the night will more than pay
The hopeless longing of the day.

Matthew Arnold (1888)

The Haunter

He does not think that I haunt him here nightly;
How shall I let him know
That whither his fancy sets him wandering
I, too, alertly go? -
Hover and hover a few feet from him
Just as I used to do,
But cannot answer the words he lifts me –
Only listen thereto!

When I could answer he did not say them:
When I could let him know
How I would like to join in his journeys
Seldom he wished to go.
Now that he goes and wants me with him
More than he used to do,
Never he sees my faithful phantom
Though he speaks thereto

Yes, I companion him to places
Only dreamers know
Where the shy hares print long paces,
Where the night rooks go;
Into old aisles where the past is all to him
Close as his shade can do,
Always lacking the power to call to him,
Near as I reach thereto

What a good haunter I am, O tell him!
Quickly make him know
If he but sigh since my loss befell him
Straight to his side I go.
Tell him a faithful one is doing
All that love can do
Still that his path may be worth pursuing,
And to bring peace thereto

Thomas Hardy (1928)

Why He Was There

Much as he left it when he went from us
Here was the room again where he had been
So long that something of him should be seen,
Or felt – and so it was. Incredulous
I turned about, loath to be greeted thus,
And there he was in his old chair, serene
As ever, and as laconic and as lean
As when he lived, and as cadaverous.

Calm as he was of old when we were young,
He sat there gazing at the pallid flame
Before him. "And how far will this go on?"
I thought. He felt the failure of my tongue,
And smiled: "I was not here until you came;
And I shall not be here when you are gone."

Edwin Arlington Robinson (1935)

Some poets write advice to their friends and relations about their own death, but on a lighter note. The advice tends towards cheerfulness and confidence either in the life hereafter or in the ongoing pleasure we should take in our lives in this world.

> Life is a great surprise I don't see why death should not be the same and even greater.
>
> *Nabokov (1968)*

> The dead don't die they look on and help
>
> *D.H.Lawrence (1930)*

> To die will be an awfully big adventure.
>
> *J.M.Barrie (1937)*

Requiem

> Under the wide and starry sky
> Dig the grave and let me lie;
> Glad did I live and gladly die,
> And I laid me down with a will.
>
> This be the verse you grave for me:
> Here he lies where he long'd to be;
> Home is the sailor, home from sea,
> And the hunter home from the hill."
>
> *Robert Louis Stevenson (1894)*

When I am dead, my dearest,
    Sing no sad songs for me;
Plant thou no roses at my head,
    Nor shady cypress tree:
Be the green grass above me
    With showers and dewdrops wet;
And if thou wilt, remember,
    And if thou wilt, forget.
I shall not see the shadows,
    I shall not feel the rain;
I shall not hear the nightingale
    Sing on, as if in pain;
And dreaming through the twilight
    That doth not rise nor set,
Haply I may remember,
    And haply may forget.

Christina Rossetti (1894)

When I have fears

When I have fears, as Keats had fears,
Of the moment I'll cease to be,
I console myself with vanished years,
Remembered laughter, remembered tears,
And the peace of the changing sea.

When I feel sad, as Keats felt sad,
That my life is so nearly done,
It gives me comfort to dwell upon
Remembered friends who are dead and gone
And the jokes we had and the fun.

How happy they are I cannot know,
But happy am I who loved them so.

Noel Coward (1973)

A Question

I asked if I got sick and died, would you
With my black funeral go walking too,
If you'd stand close to hear them talk or pray
While I am let down in that steep bank of clay.
And, No, you said, for if you saw a crew
Of living idiots, pressing round the new
Oak coffin - they alive, I dead beneath
That board, - you'd rave and rend them with
                              your teeth.

J.M.Synge (1909)

Silence, solitude, loneliness, all these interweave, come and go, sometimes bringing peace, sometimes not. Henri Nouwen, a contemplative monk, in his work on *Solitude and Loneliness* gives this advice about adapting to being alone, if we also value the life of the spirit.

> Instead of running away from our loneliness...
> we have to protect it and turn it into a fruitful
> solitude. To live the spiritual life we must first find
> the courage to enter the desert of our loneliness and
> to change it by gentle and persistent effort into a
> garden of solitude.

But the silence in the mind
is when we live best, within
listening distance of the silence
we call God. This is the deep
calling to deep of the psalm-
writer, the bottomless ocean
we launch the armada of
our thoughts on, never arriving.

It is a presence, then,
whose margins are our margins;
that calls us out over our
own fathoms. What to do
but draw a little nearer to
such ubiquity by remaining still?

R.S.Thomas (2000)

This World is not Conclusion

This World is not Conclusion.
A Species stands beyond—
Invisible, as Music—
But positive, as Sound—
It beckons, and it baffles—
Philosophy—don't know—
And through a Riddle, at the last—
Sagacity, must go—
To guess it, puzzles scholars—
To gain it, Men have borne
Contempt of Generations
And Crucifixion, shown—
Faith slips—and laughs, and rallies—

Blushes, if any see—
Plucks at a twig of Evidence—
And asks a Vane, the way—
Much Gesture, from the Pulpit—
Strong Hallelujahs roll—
Narcotics cannot still the Tooth
That nibbles at the soul—

Emily Dickinson (1886)

If the doors of perception were cleared everything
would appear to man as it is, infinite

William Blake (1827)

Following is a small selection of specifically Christian verse; the first
one is by a man who was a chaplain to the armed forces in W.W.I.
His poems were mostly written in the context of the war so he knew
about pain and loss.

My Peace I Give Unto You

Blessed are the eyes that see
    The things that you have seen,
Blessed are the feet that walk
    The ways where you have been.
Blessed are the eyes that see
    The Agony of God,
Blessed are the feet that tread
    The path His feet have trod.

Blessed are the souls that solve
    The paradox of Pain,
And find the path that, piercing it,
    Lead through to Peace again.

G.A. Studdert Kennedy (1929)

Grant to life's day a calm unclouded ending,
   An eve untouched by shadows of decay:
The brightness of a holy death-bed blending
   With dawning glories of the eternal day.

St. Ambrose (397)

Just Another Death

Who can understand death? You ogre. There's
nothing one can conceal about death. Yes, the
parlours can sanitize, make a palm-fringed sanctuary
for the body.
They can take it away.

You ogre, you sit grinning. I'm glad to know you're
beaten. He isn't here. Oh, I grant you the shape, the
tidy shell – his wisp of hair, his gentle mask of face.
But I know you are beaten. And if I can't exactly
laugh, there's some point to holding a wake. I'll sing
and dance to hide my grief.

And somewhere, unfettered, his laugh, his quiet
remark, hovers over the funeral parlour, the as yet
unmarked grave.

Mary Dilworth

O Come Quickly!

Never weather-beaten sail more willing to shore,
Never tired pilgrim's limbs affected slumber more,
Than my wearied spirit now longs to fly out of my
troubled breast
O come quickly, sweetest Lord, and take my soul to
                                            rest!
Ever blooming are the joys of heaven's high
                                    Paradise,
Cold age deals not there our ears, nor vapour dims
                                    our eyes:
Glory there the sun outshines; whose beams the
                                    Blesséd only see
O come quickly, sweetest Lord, and raise my sprite
                                    to Thee!

Thomas Campion (1619)

In this famous Holy Sonnet John Donne (1631) addresses Death
itself; echoing St. Paul, he claims Christ's victory over death:

Death be not proud

Death be not proud, though some have called thee
Mighty and dreadful, for, thou art not so,
For, those, whom thou think'st, thou dost overthrow,
Die not, poor death, nor yet canst thou kill me.
From rest and sleep, which but thy pictures bee,
Much pleasure, then from thee, much more
                                    must flow,
And soonest our best men with thee doe go,

Rest of their bones and souls delivery.
Thou are slave to Fate, Chance, kings and
                              desperate men.
And dost with poison, war, and sickness dwell,
And poppy, or charms can make us sleep as well,
And better than thy stroke; why swell'st thou then?
One short sleep past, wee wake eternally,
And death shall be no more; death, thou shalt die

At the round earth's imagin'd corners

At the round earth's imagin'd corners, blow
Your trumpets, Angel, and arise, arise
From death, you numberless infinities
Of souls, and to your scattered bodies go,
All whom the flood did and fire shall o'erthrow,
All whom war, dearth, age, agues, tyrannies,
Despair, law, chance, hath slain, and you whose eyes
Shall behold God, and never taste deaths woe.
But let them sleep, Lord, and me mourn a space,
For if above all these, my sins abound,
'Tis late to ask abundance of thy grace,
When wee are there; here on this lowly ground,
Teach me how to repent; for that's as good
As if thou hadst seal'd my pardon, with thy blood.

John Donne

And death shall have no dominion

St. Paul and Dylan Thomas.

Finally a few poems to ponder as one begins to consider that life might go on. The first three are from Tagore

Delusions I did cherish

Delusions I did cherish but now I am rid of them.
Tracing the track of false hopes I trod upon thorns to know that they are not flowers.
I shall never trifle with love,
Never play with heart
I shall find my refuge in you
On the shore of the troubled sea.

I was walking along a path overgrown with grass,
when suddenly I heard from some one behind,
"See if you know me?"
    I turned round and looked at her and said,
"I cannot remember your name."
    She said, "I am that first great Sorrow whom you met when you were young."
    Her eyes looked like a morning whose dew is sill in the air
    I stood silent for some time till I said, "Have you lost all the great burden of your tears?"
    She smiled and said nothing. I felt that her tears had had time to learn the language of smiles.
    "Once you said," she whispered, "that you would cherish your grief for ever."

I blushed and said, "Yes, but years have passed and I forget."

Then I took her hand in mine and said, "But you have changed."

"What was sorrow once has now become peace," she said.

I will meet one day

I will meet one day the Life within me, the Joy that hides in my life, though the days perplex my path with their idle dust.
I have known it in glimpses, and its fitful breath has come upon me making my thoughts fragrant for a while.
I will meet one day the Joy without me that dwells behind the screen of light – and will stand in the overflowing solitude where all things are seen as by their creator.

Evolution

Out of the dusk a shadow,
Then a spark;
Out of the cloud a silence,
Then a lark;
Out of the heart a rapture
Then a pain;
Out of the dead, cold ashes,
Life again.

John Bannister Tabb (1909)

Arrival

Not conscious
    that you have been seeking
        suddenly
    you come upon it

the village in the Welsh hills
        dust free
    with no road out
but the one you came in by.

      A bird chimes
    from a green tree
the hour that is no hour
    you know. The river dawdles
to hold a mirror for you
where you may see yourself
    as you are, a traveller
        with the moon's halo
    above him, who has arrived
    after long journeying where he
        began, catching this
    one truth by surprise
that there is everything to look forward to.

R S Thomas (2000)

Love After Love

The time will come
when, with elation,
you will greet yourself arriving
at your own door, in your own mirror,
and each will smile at the other's welcome,

and say sit here. Eat.
You will love again the stranger who was your self,
Give wine. Give bread. Give back your heart
to itself, to the stranger who has loved you

all your life, whom you ignored
for another, who knows you by heart.
Take down the love-letters from the bookshelf

the photographs, the desperate notes,
peel your own image from the mirror.
Sit. Feast on your life.

Derek Walcott

LOVE AND DEATH

We must be still and still moving
Into another intensity
For a further union, a deeper communion
Through the dark cold and the empty desolation

T.S.Eliot: Four Quartets East Coker V

That love is stronger than death has been a deeply embedded belief in my system always. It is beyond question. A second belief, equally beyond question is that life goes on beyond physical death. These truths I knew and trusted. Always. They did not assuage the pain of my husband's death, but in some ways they helped me find meaning in the meaningless and, of course, kept me open to the possibilities of continued communication. I know that such a statement leaves me open to the accusation of self-delusion. Whatever one says from a point of subjective experience is open to contradiction and perhaps ridicule from an unbeliever bent on 'objectivity'. I know all the arguments and have run through them many times. I do not mind that not everyone would accept the reality of my experiences; they were real, outside my control, as I shall show. If on the final day I find that I was indeed mistaken, I shall not mind that either since the belief system on which I organise my life makes more sense to me than any other, so I choose it, with a certain peppering of agnosticism which saves me from sentimentality.

This chapter is decidedly personal and shares something of my own experience of grief and evidence of the Beyond in the hope that it may enliven, even for the odd moment, another's pain. It may, too encourage some people to be open to the possibilities of 'the further reaches of human nature'. Sometimes, reading of another's pain is all one can take; this is why I have shared a little of my long night- sea voyage.

Because writing is what I do when the going gets rough there are pieces from the past that move me now, but I know that I could not have written them now. I share them in the hope that the flotsam and the bits of driftwood from my wreckage might give others even a temporary hold on their own way through the long night. When things are really awful for me the words come out 'more poetic-like', necessary, but not good poetry! I have included some of the verse writing because it captures the feelings of the moment, most especially the despair that overtakes one from time to time, and that not only in the beginning; some of the verse is of much later date.

If I were to write on grief from my present perspective I would, some of the time, be writing from the memory of various phases of grief. To describe those phases or make plain what they were like the words must come from the moment, not the memory of the moment.

I have said before that grief partakes of the nature of eternity so that suddenly and unaccountably, at any time, one can be pierced by the grief so poignant that once again it feels like 'only yesterday'. This moment occurs in the midst of life but in the beginning there is no life to be in the midst of, one is only enveloped by the silence, the numbness and the pain.

LOVE AND DEATH

These two pieces that follow I could not write now. I remember what it felt like, but, of course, my perspective is changed. The constancy of pain and the futility of going on are not as they once were; the poignancy has mellowed.

> Madame Grief is a capricious lover, variable, always unpredictable, she can be tender, torrid or tempestuous and inordinately demanding. She will not suffer her dues to be conditioned or contained in neat boxes or the stages that clever people designate for her. As the stages of labour may be useful for monitors observing a birth but supremely irrelevant to the chief actors in the drama, so with grief and death, the actuals are too pressing, the life imperative too all-consuming for categories to matter at all.

> There is that common reading at weddings from *The Prophet* about trees growing up side by side, not entwined. All makes sense but now, without the tree growing beside me I know I have to go on alone, but why? The problem is in not having any desire. I don't want to do what it takes. What for? That's the big question. When we were working and growing together there was some sort of goal. Now death is my only goal. I have no other meaningful goal to strive for.

In the most unlikely places we can find words that capture our own experience. This piece comes from a detective story, *The Shortest Way to Hades* and it captures beautifully what Jung means by 'the night-sea journey' when the darkness seems limitless and we cannot conceive of it being otherwise.

The darkness of a night at sea with no moon and no stars isn't like being in a room with the light shut out; the sea is black and the sky is black, so there is no horizon, and the darkness has no limit to it.

Sarah Caudwell: The Shortest Way to Hades

I count myself fortunate that, as I believed in life after death, the intimations of B, though surprising, were not wholly unexpected; what was surprising was the recognition that such contact was important to him. Previously I had believed that any communication from Beyond, (where ever that might be) was to comfort, console or even inform the bereaved. Through these experiences I discovered that there was more to it than that.

Just a word on that question of 'where ever that might be': some writers have talked of the departed as 'only in the next room'; others, historically, have given more elaborate definitions of whereabouts and the progress on the Other Side, along with a timetable for the progress. There seems to me to be a tendency to impose earthly time and space onto a realm where such things do not exist, so we must admit to using metaphor rather than definition. I heard in a science programme once, of the man who first discovered the eleventh dimension, he described it as "closer to us than the clothes on our bodies". That struck me as a good metaphor for the Beyond. The ordinary, untrained person can no more conceive of the other dimensions of which science speaks than we can conceive of Eternity.

Question: Where does the soul go when it dies?
Answer: There is no need for it to go anywhere.

Jacob Boeheme (1624)

I said I believed that to B whether I am here or there doesn't matter because he couldn't love me more or be closer to me either way – somehow in that loving we participate in eternity: a love story without end. However, the experiences of his continuing presence were and still are sometimes startling, always unexpected, but real and undeniable. For me the strongest proof has been in my inability to 'conjure him', as Shakespeare would call it. When I was at my lowest, when I would have done anything to be able to feel his presence he simply was not there, he never has come at my bidding. On the other hand, in the midst of thinking about something else, being busy or doing nothing, I can suddenly feel his 'there-ness' so strongly. Other people have documented similar experiences. C.S.Lewis in a *Grief Observed* describes his experiences in this way:

> For I have discovered passionate grief does not
> link us with the dead but cuts us off from them
> this becomes clearer and clearer. It is just at those
> moments when I feel least sorrow - getting into
> my morning bath is one of them - that H rushes
> upon my mind in her full reality, her otherness.
> Not, as in my worst moments, or foreshortened and
> patheticized and solemnized by my own miseries,
> but as she is in her own right. This is good and tonic.

The family's first intimation of his continuing presence was indeed startling. This is the background story: Way back in the seventies B had a dear friend who was dying. He spent a great deal of time at the hospital, sharing with and ministering to his friend who was an artist of some repute. Before his death the friend directed B to a gallery where one of his pictures was hanging. The curator had been instructed to give it to B as a memento of the artist's love and gratitude. All this went according to plan and soon after this the friend died. In succeeding years, long after we left the parish in which we had been ministering at the time, B was startled and distressed to find himself accused of stealing this picture from the church. As a man who could not tolerate his honour being impugned he allowed the painting to be taken back to the church. We hung a different picture in its spot and that was that; a story sad but true.

In the third night after his going from us there was a terrible bang, crash and a shattering of glass. The picture that had hung safely for a decade or more was cast down from the wall. I had a fantasy of the friend greeting B on the Other Side, and asking why he had allowed his gift to be so abused! In due course the painting was restored to us and B's honour was cleared.

My journal records in the first months of bereavement what it was like "living in an awful shaky, scary, alone feeling. I am abandoned in a dark and silent universe." Grief is not linear. The notes are fitful, jumpy; showing painfully what it is like trying to come to terms with reality, when there is no stability; being resigned and resentful by turns; being sure of his ongoing presence and doubting it the next minute. I tell myself:

> I should be still, feeding myself on poetry, actually doing the things I know, after, I will wish that I had. When I just live the emptiness I gain a kind of stillness. This is an opportunity to clear my mind and create a new state of being that will allow me to live as I want to. I have to practice living in that state of mind now, letting my mind be fed by the poetry I read. "I said to my soul be still....." But after an evening, night and morning on my own I am faced

with what life is going to be like for as long as I live.
When the silence is only silence what a yawning
gap of emptiness lies before me. Though I know that
he is there I have to find myself peaceful separate
from him.

Then there are days when peacefulness is not possible:

Today I just want B; I want him here and I want him
here now. I know more strongly than ever that he is
here with me but I'd rather be there with him. I have
to get back into the world. I recoil. I have no desire
to speak to anyone, to re-join the human race. I just
wish I too were dead.

Sometimes I have a strong, yet frustrating sense of B's
presence at other times there is only the question
"am I kidding myself?" I don't think so. Death Come
Soon.

Then maybe even the next day: I cannot catch even
a whiff of B: his silence deafens me and yet the 'bat-
squeak' is there, barely heard, but just enough to
make denial of his presence complete. I am grateful
for that.

As the New Year came in my writing became a little more
thoughtful, more frequently it was in the nature of dialogue. There
seemed to be more of him to share and more of my deliberations
on the meaning of this life I ded not want to live. On the first day of
the new millennium I can say: B is more and more apparent to me
as the days go by so I am achieving some sort of equilibrium.
Yesterday we had a profound conversation in which he said to my
re-iterated complaint of his dying, that I was missing the point.

He said that we all fail to realise on this side the truth that this life is only a preparation for the one that he now lives in; the quest for consciousness is the most important work to do in this life.

Soon however the sense of confusion once more takes over: I do not feel B with me in the ways that I have over the past week, but I do still have the sense of him trying to tell me something that I cannot quite hear.

The necessity of getting back into normal life starts to make itself felt and brings its own dilemma. If I take up life once more will it mean that I lose this connection which seems like the only thing that truly matters? 'Memory be green' might have been my motto at this time, I so did not want to get on with life, but life seemed to want to get on with me.

> If I give up mourning our shared life I am scared
> he will desert me and that I will lose what little
> (?) connection I have. His voice drums in my ears
> in contradiction. Hanging on means I only have
> memory, moving on means I have him – this he says
> to me and explodes at my 'little'. He seems to say our
> on-going connection is anything but that! I am scared
> that if I get back into life I will dilute or lose the desire
> to die and then have to live a long time and get old
> (without him). However I do not want to give in to a
> state of perpetual mourning which robs life of any
> scrap of meaning. Dreaming about B gives me hope
> – gives me life – suggests to me that perhaps I can live
> in a new space with him – but I have got to do my bit.
> And then I sit in a quiet space and Love envelopes me.

I found this verse somewhere just when I needed it, then I said it each night before sleep:

> Come to me in my dreams, and then
> By day I shall be well again
> For so the night will more than pay
> The hopeless longing of the day.

Matthew Arnold

In March I moved into a new home. Some friends were helping me move, bearing all the paraphernalia that goes along with a total house move. As I went to go inside I found on the door-step a very jolly photo of B on the day we had moved into our last home, nearly twenty years before. I do not know where it had come from; we were not carrying photo albums or any such in. It was a strong re-assurance to me that he wanted me to know he was coming with me into my new abode. However, the sense of his being there was no more consistent and always raised the question of whether his apparent disappearance was due to my lack of attention, or of serenity, or whether the withdrawal was from his side.

> It occurs to me today that the other world is so far
> beyond our experience and understanding that
> any contact we have with it will be interpreted, by
> us, in terms of what we think we know, and what
> we believe about life. That's why the differences are
> so great. If George Appleton is right and "Silence is
> the language of Eternity", it would explain why the
> mystics have a deeper understanding because they
> know the language and are practiced in it – the rest
> of us have to make our meaning out of the silence.

Loneliness or silence
Silence is being quietly at home with B
Loneliness is being home alone.

The silence never seems to get less arduous and
the restoration never less surprising: When I sit in
the quiet there is just complete blankness where,
at other times, I've been aware of B. I have sat here
for an hour, v. calm, v. still, v. blank. It is not a dark,
unpleasant feeling but it is as though I am in an ante-
room, waiting, barred from entering into something
that would satisfy and heal. I don't know what to do.

It is 25 WEEKS TODAY! How different life is when
you come back! Suddenly in the garden yesterday
he was there again. C.S.L calls it the "apprehension
of intelligence" like one-ness and separation at the
same time. I lay in bed this morning embraced in
this. It was daylight (maybe it was a trick of the
light) but with my eyes closed I kept experiencing
a burning brightness and my body felt enveloped,
'suffused with love'. Nothing of this experience
was memory.

The next milestone was collecting his Ashes from the cemetery.
I needed to do this on my own and on the way there I had a curious
experience. Before ever I met B, when we lived in adjoining flatlets I
used to hear him singing, he always sang in the shower, and in those
days he usually sang, "On the street where you live". His favourite
male jazz vocalist was always Mel Tormé. Driving to the cemetery
that day, feeling very, very frail I put the radio on to distract myself
and on came M.T. singing "On the street where you live" I have never
heard that track before or since. It felt quite weird but it helped me
through that day.

I was quite proud of myself for managing this effort:
I did it! I collected that wee parcel from the cemetery
into which your luscious body has been shaped and
you said "That wasn't my luscious body; that had
wasted and dissolved long before". I feel this pull
towards you, like we are both reaching out but an
impenetrable barrier keeps us apart. You tell me
to let go, stop straining, and accept love. I am filled
once more with such sweetness.

It is clear from the notes that as the months go by I was processing
and thinking through what this all meant; how to live with constancy
and trust in the reality of our continuing relationship. Increasingly
the notes record dialogue. This is now April of the first year:

Today is your birthday. This is what I believe: That
if human beings have consciousness and there is a
consciousness or soul reality that endures beyond
the grave then it must be possible to live in/with
that greater reality and discover on this side a way
of relating to the other side that makes sense and
is intelligible and rewarding and fulfilling while
still in the flesh – otherwise I don't see the point.
I'd be much happier if I could find the way to live
constantly in the state of awareness. As soon as I
connect with other people it is lost.

The books we read before you died did not have a wide
enough, deep enough context. "This was my path,"
you said. You are sorry for my pain but you know the
rightness of how things are now; we have work to do.
What's more you will not be waiting for me to come to
you because you will be with me all the way.

You seem always to be wanting me to see that your view of life is superior to mine. I believe you but will not falsify my own need and deny my longing for all the lovely loving, laughing reality of your physical presence. Instantly my whole body is filled with such uncommon sweetness and for a time it feels as though this could overwhelm the 'lesser' longing of which I complained. You want me to believe more and treasure the silent communication which can grow even more beautiful. This is a joy and a frustration. Maybe one day I will have evolved far enough to have diminished the frustration.

I sit in the quiet for ages – but I do not find you with me – I find only my longing, my bewilderment and loneliness. I keep telling myself you will be back; I keep worrying that the time of your loving presence with me is over.

I cannot doubt the evidence of my own senses. You were with me again tonight. After such absence in which I felt that you had gone for good, you'd never really 'been' or that I'd constructed you out of my own need – all this went out of the window in the simple extreme fact that you were once more with me. The staggering thing was that you were there loving me because you wanted to be not simply as a way of bringing comfort to me.

> Not where I breathe but where
> I love, I live.

> *Robert Southwell*

LOVE AND DEATH

We talked about why he left me. He didn't fancy 'old' or 'invalid'; didn't fancy me having to sacrifice my life to looking after him. I love him, I'd rather have had him thus than not at all. He doesn't agree, thinks what we have now is better. I don't feel that way today.

Yellow roses have always been special for me and he often gave them to me and it seems he did again because one night there was a yellow rose blown off a bush in the back garden, in the morning it was lying at the front door! These things defy rational explanation; that the breeze should blow it over the house and onto the doormat is highly unlikely and there was no-one else around to perform the task. The non-rational explanation ends up being the most likely.

There is a strain about adjusting to life with other people. Life goes on for them naturally and more easily that it does for me. I felt the burden of this, on the one hand not wanting to be boring or embarrassing and on the other wanting to be true to how I felt and to what was real for me. There was nothing but loving consideration from my family but I felt bad about not giving more care and attention to them and their feelings.

> Big crying night. Suddenly I am bored with all this
> pretending to a life. This is no life and I want to be
> real about that; pretending so as not to be a bore
> to other people is getting me down. There is such a
> strong sense of everyone being very careful with me,
> concerned, but not wanting to open 'Pandora's Box'. I
> think in spite of myself I am becoming so habituated
> to being alone that I become exhausted by constant
> inter-action with other people

I saw my Chinese healer today. She said I was in 'grief madness' in my mind. Being so unfocussed it is not surprising if I don't behave very rationally. Then again I came into a quiet place after some time. He told me he had waited for me. He reminded me that he had said, "Keep your eyes on me and I will pull you through."

In August of that first year the girls and I met for dinner, the first time since he left us that we had shared a meal, just the five of us. We used the table settings that signified family celebration but before dinner I silently bemoaned to him that he was not there. He assured me he would be. Suddenly, during the meal one of the dinner plates broke in two. I told him that was not a comfortable assurance of his presence, but it did emphasise that the sixth plate was no longer needed!

By the end of the first year I was still very fragile and the misery had not abated. In spite of so much evidence of his being around there was continual doubt of him staying 'available'. The apprehension of his presence alternated with the overwhelming sense of his absence. "If I don't go over into despair I can stay close to him. When I am quietly here on my own with him I am more at ease."

Today is the Anniversary of you leaving. Whatever else I am doing I am participating in the mystery that is us. In the pitch dark of the room I said, "You feel so close I should be able to see you." Then, on the wall, directly in front of me there was this dancing ball of light. Everything around it was pitch dark. It hovered there for about 10 minutes then gradually faded. I don't know whether it was he or not. At the time it certainly felt like it.

Today is a sitting and staring into space day, a what-in-the-world-is-the-point day. I can't find B. There is just this aching loss and numbness, a hole where once there was a sense of Presence. Sometimes, like now, I feel I cannot go on. Quite happily, by the end of the day I'd decided to die in my sleep, (a bit of my mind also doubted) perhaps the answer is to be simple with no doubts.

Sparks

Each evening as I close my eye
I pray the Lord that I might die
And every morning when I wake,
sadly: *My soul He did not take.*

A friend I had once, who
when, life so sad, knew
how to lie down on his bed
and days later be found
- dead.

Dear Sparks what secret code had you
to quit so simply?
I wish I knew.

I was trying to remember the book I'd promised myself to look out. He said, "Silent Music". I said it wasn't that and kept looking. Finally I opened his recommendation, at random, to chapter II which concludes with some wonderful stuff on love as the way to enlightenment or resurrection. This is what I was looking for:

> (Spiritual friendship) a total and unitive silence
> enjoying one another in love
>
> *William Johnson: Silent Music*

In November I was doing a Retreat. I couldn't find him, I thought
perhaps he wasn't accustomed to coming with me on retreat.
However, in the chapel, I found his Presence again, briefly but so
sharply. This time he came through scent! I was sitting in the quiet
when suddenly there was this whiff of him, quite unmistakeable
and distinct from all the other chapel smells. After a few minutes it
wasn't there, but my heart was light again.

> I cry: What's it all for, it is all so meaningless, so
> pointless. He says, "You can't say the work we are
> engaged on is meaningless". And then I cry some
> more. I know I must learn the language of this
> silence. I ask about the future – where do we go from
> here and you tell me only deeper and deeper into
> the silence of loving. That's what eternity is. And is
> it enough? Well, there ain't anythin' else and it has
> been enough for countless millions.
> If only...... if only! I think of things we might have
> done differently and he says, "It wouldn't have made
> any difference. I would still have died on that day." "Is
> the day of everyone's death appointed?" I ask. "As far
> as I know", he seemed to say.

The first year of grieving was over. The communication, the grief,
the writing all continued and eventually a new stability was
established, but it took a long time. The times of a trustful serenity
gradually became more constant, but not because of any conscious
act on my part. Throughout, it was imperative for me to allow

things to take a natural course. I refused to coerce myself into ways of being that were false. Eventually I became interested in life once again and ceased to long for an early death. The poems I wrote through these years indicate how slow the process was, for me. I wrote lots of poems, it was a useful way of ordering my feelings and expressing the pain and sadness that I could not speak of to anyone.

It seems to be one of the universal aspects of grieving, that after a time one feels one cannot speak about the pain, it is unseemly, sort of embarrassing. Within the family it would be a source of further pain, to speak feelingly of the experience. Each member has their own grief to deal with, so making reference, "I had a bit of a bad day yesterday" is as much as one gives out generally. Poetry, both reading and writing was a form of solace. These few poems give an insight into the progress, and sometimes the lack of it!

This Great Sadness (2001)

This great Sadness has no other name
But Grief.
Grief
Is an absolute meaning
It cannot be explained in terms of anything else.
Grief is

Not to be controlled, corrected or cured.
Grief only can be lived, accepted; waited upon
Grief, I presume has its own parameters unknown to
the conscious mind.

However it is, grief will have its way.
Our part is to bear it willingly,
content to be sad, uncomplaining.

However much we want to kick against the truth
Grief is.
Sadness is
as much a part of life as breathing. So what?

Crying (2001)

...and if there is crying,
cry
without reason, excuse or explanation
And certainly without apology.
Cry like Niobe
because grief is what it is
and tears will have their way.

Trigg Island Café - Desperate (May 2001)

I heard of a girl dead
next door to her parents' flat
by her own hand.
"What family's that," they said,
"that a girl could suffer so and be not known?"
But, oh, I know, I know
The familiar expectation of revival:
Sad mood, bad mood; no more
Fond families, respectful, going about their days
missing the tokens of despair
Unaware of the impulse: the swift suggestive acts
that lean towards the end.

June (2001)

A past laden with laughter
        and loving tenderness.

A past of desire, engagement, passion
        and loving kindness

Prolonged infinitely.

A future undesired, unattended
        postponed – indefinitely.
Be still, be calm
                'And all shall be well...'

On my side it doesn't look like a prison

A walled garden, rather old fashioned flowers
Hollyhocks and foxgloves, larkspur and peonies
brace the wall
Colourful, alluring and yet I know
On the other side there is more.

Calling: sublime, silent, enticing
And imperative.

I long to come.

If there is a gate,
- aperture of any kind
I cannot find it.
If ever there was a gate
flowers have covered it long ago.
No place now
Where I can broach the wall
And dissolve in the ecstasy beyond.

Today (February 2009)

I want to cry the dry,
arid, comfortless cry.

Once again my life has
Scrunched in the act
of intelligent management
and descended on the hot dead leaves
    into self-boredom;
    rancid, implausible.
A no-man's land where
each presenting possibility
is smothered in a blanket of disaffection.

LOVE AND DEATH

One tires of the deceit, or the pride of managing
well.

For myself I have to stop sometimes
- being splendid.

In the quiet of my home, being honest with myself
comes haltingly and with difficulty.
Permission to admit I would if I could, cry.

There is a key
I know there is a key

I feel it; there is something I cannot quite see
The key to unlock some hitherto unknown,
                unrecognised resource to free me
And send me forward
with sustainable self-worth –
knowledge, genuine desire.

The inner value that
makes loneliness
solitude

I do not want company...
I want that opening up; the revelation
that awakens me, for more than just a moment,
to a life that isn't "nothing but..."
to joy, vision, laughter and...
Something more,
Enduring.

I-can't-be-bothered (August 2011)

I-can't-be-bothered
has a second line:

What's the point?

No-one to appreciate, encourage, enjoy.
There will be no praise
and neither will there be blame.
But

If I don't be bothered enough
I might suffer the fate of horror:
To be given over into other hands to be
                              bothered for me.
If they are also bothered by me they will drug me
                              to the eyeballs.
And I'd never bother anyone, ever again.

All Hallow's Eve (2011)

All Hallow's Eve.
A satisfactory day to conclude
Pondering October.

A satisfactory day to close the book.

There is something strange about October

But there is something strange about October
Indelible memory, too deep for words?
Like the sunken cathedral,
Slumbering; archaic intimations annually stirred?

Resounding echoes of the bell rung in the tenth
month of every year?

Memory resurrects to pain
events, sadness, regrets:
"My God, that too was October"

Yes, October has brought
horror, pain, and tensions past understanding.

If, as the poet says, past and future
are eternally present,
memory, free from the constraints of time
is not restricted to history.

If past and future are both present,
in those years of light
when October's shadow fell over the days did it
indeed point back to archaic layers or
forward to the cataclysm that was to come?

St. Francis' Day in Ninety-nine
Was horror enough for all of time –
my time, forwards, or backwards.

There is something strange about October.

Now, after all this time, it continues to be the case that days before
significant dates, anniversaries, and birthdays, for example, I am
subdued and need to be quiet and reflective. When his five women
are together inexplicable happenings still occur. Things which may,
with a stretch, be explained as extraordinary coincidences, but they
are so unusual that to find a rational explanation is more convoluted
than the non-rational. It does seem as though, somehow, he is
making the point that he is still part of the family.

After so many years, this is an unfinished story and I can still suddenly be hit by the 'it-only-happened-yesterday' feeling that knocks me sideways for a while. The loneliness and loss can still unhinge but with less persistence or urgency and, on the other hand, the communication continues. When he was here in the flesh, no matter what he, or I, were attending to, in the same house or many miles apart, reading, thinking, attending to the needs of others, we were always together - bonded at such depth that it didn't require editing or defining. That's what marriage is.

Now we seem to be much the same. No longer is it a case of, "now he is here –now he is not", but rather there is the knowing we dwell in love and 'here and now cease to matter'. I can turn my attention solely to him and be warmed by the connection or I can go about my day, not thinking about him because I do not have to be thinking about him to be connected. There is the silence. The language of eternity is silence; communication does not come in sentences but in apprehension. In the beginning words were necessary, but there comes a time when they are redundant and the exchange is more direct, *'the total and unitive silence'* as William Johnson called it.

> And what the dead had no speech for, when living,
> They can tell you, being dead: the communication
> Of the dead is tongued with fire beyond the language
> of the living

T.S. Eliot: Four Quartets Little Gidding I

I made some notes on this way back in July 2000 after a conversation with B:

Tongues of fire represent heavenly inspiration.
Love is the basis for heavenly inspiration.
Love and fire are one.

The language we, the living, cannot understand is
the language of love. Fire, (especially in this poem) is
the means of purification and so the language of love
that is beyond us is the love that has been purified
by fire. The fire has burned away all the earthly
trappings, hang-ups or concerns; the pure essential
loving self remains. This language is beyond us.

I believe too that it is a language where more is
conveyed in silence than in speech. I am shockingly
verbal. I like things said, spelled out. This
communication of the dead is spelled out in silence.
I have to translate some of it into English in order
to know that I've 'got it'. Sometimes he does it in
English, I guess for the same reason.

I have flashes of knowing, but then I scatter and
find it hard to restore myself. I guess at these times I
am filled with that communication and it is almost
too much for me to bear. I have to let my mind go
somewhere else. I create a kind of muffler; suddenly
it is all padded around with cotton waste and I
cannot find nor can I hear the resonances that were
there before. I must trust that it will come back.

Happily it always will; it always has!

TIME FOR A STORY

Once upon a time, through a strange country, there rode some goodly knights, and their path lay by a deep wood, where tangled briars grew very thick and strong, and tore the flesh of them that lost their way therein. And the leaves of the trees that grew in the wood were very dark and thick, so that no ray of light came through the branches to lighten the gloom and sadness.

And, as they passed by that dark wood, one knight of those that rode, missing his comrades, wandered far away, and returned to them no more; and they, sorely grieving, rode on without him, mourning him as one dead.

Now, when they reached the fair castle towards which they had been journeying, they stayed there many days, and made merry; and one night, as they sat in cheerful ease around the logs that burned in the great hall and drank a loving measure, there came the comrade they had lost, and greeted them. His clothes were ragged, like a beggar's, and many sad wounds were on his sweet flesh, but upon his face there shone a great radiance of deep joy.

And they questioned him, asking him what had befallen him: and he told them how in the dark wood he had lost his way, and had wandered many days and nights, till, torn and bleeding, he had lain him down to die.

Then, when he was nigh unto death, lo! through the savage gloom there came to him a stately maiden, and took him by the hand and led him on through devious paths, unknown to any man, until upon the darkness of the wood there dawned a light such as the light of day was unto but as a little lamp unto the sun; and, in that wondrous light, our way-worn knight saw as in a dream a vision, and so glorious, so fair the vision seemed, that of his bleeding wounds he thought no more, but stood as one entranced, whose joy is as deep as is the sea, whereof no man can tell the depth.

And the vision faded, and the knight, kneeling upon the ground, thanked the good saint who into that sad wood had strayed his steps, so he had seen the vision that lay there hid.

And the name of the dark forest was Sorrow; but of the vision that the good knight saw therein we may not speak nor tell.

From *Three Men in a Boat by Jerome K. Jerome (1927)*

FURTHER REACHES
– ANOTHER SHORE

I must be willing to give up what I am in order to become what I will be

Albert Einstein

We understand death to be both an end and a beginning for the one who dies, (if one believes in the Life Hereafter). It is the end of life in the flesh and the beginning of life in another dimension, 'on another shore and in a greater light' so it is both death and birth. It has not often been shown that for the ones left behind it can also be a new birth, on the further side of the death, which is also our 'little death'. With stillness, dedication and being real about what is going on for us we can achieve a new way of being that transcends the life we lived before. We must, to some extent, avoid being pulled aside by life's many distractions if we are to find a meaningful life beyond what we are now enduring. Of course, we will welcome distraction, but if life becomes only avoidance, by medical or by social means, we miss the opportunity to grow into the fullness that is our potential.

There are ways in which we can aid this work, once we are sufficiently stable to consider 'what next?' Keeping a journal is, for many people, a great way to chart one's course. One can keep track of the ups and the downs and be able to observe the patterns of our grieving, to see where, emotionally, we have come from and how we have changed.

Having a mentor, guide or confidante, who is not family or friend involved in their own grief, is a huge help. This needs to be someone who understands, who can listen without the need either to jolly one along or feel they have some responsibility to 'put things right'. Professionals may treat us clinically, as 'a case' that needs to be returned to normality. Our friends tend to want to be helpful or they are frightened to hear what we need to express; this is why someone 'outside' can be most useful. We need someone who simply listens, when we need to talk. It is not easy to find someone we get on with who has these qualifications, but it is of enormous value and worth the search.

It may be 'old hat', but I have to re-iterate that there is no substitute for a spot of exercise. Making sure we walk regularly, if we have no other familiar form of physical exercise makes a world of difference. The desire and tendency to 'moulder' is very strong and it takes a spot of will-power to begin to give our body what it needs, but it is worth the effort.

Reading is another way in which we can aid our progress. There is a huge body of literature from various fields of study, that deals with the issues of life, death, grief and the life Beyond. What follows is very small selection of writings that I hope has the virtue of being consoling and inspiring and suggestive of tracks you might find interesting or useful to follow.

> The unhappiness of the current stage of human
> development stems from the fact that, for the most
> part, we do not yet 'see' the reality to which both
> science and intuition point. We are caught in a
> hollow where the fog still enshrouds us; we still have
> far to go on our journey towards the high places.

Darryl Reanney

This quote has been one of the most meaningful images for me since I first read it years ago. It comes from a book called *The Death of Forever* by a molecular biologist, Dr Darryl Reanney (1994). I find Reanney's explorations of human consciousness and the meaning of death inspiring and as thrilling as they are free from cant. He wrote as a scientist, deeply spiritual, but not specifically Christian, he also understood that poetry is a means of communicating truth that reaches beyond the surface of our language. He found in the poetry of T.S. Eliot intuitive insights which corresponded particularly to the theories of quantum physics. Only rarely do we find a scientist of his calibre taking seriously the issues of death and beyond and writing so lucidly and encouragingly.

In an interview towards the end of his life Dr Reanney stated his belief that the deep insights of modern science validate in quite profound ways the sacred and historic traditions, the prime example being the understanding of the Oneness of all things.

> I had seen birth and death,
> But had thought they were different; this Birth was
> Hard and bitter agony for us, like Death, our death.

T.S. Eliot: The Journey of the Magi

Reanney was passionate in his belief that grief could be a journey. This journey that is imposed on us by the death of a loved one can take us from the 'little' death we suffer at the loss, though indeed it does not seem 'little' while we endure it, to a new stable state which is birth into a new way of being. However, there is no easy way through:

> The unpalatable aspect of this is the inevitable requirement for hardship as a precondition of human growth, of the evolution of human consciousness

But though this birth may be 'hard and bitter agony for us' the result can be profound:

> The death of the old is the birth of the new and the new self, the new stable state into which the lessened ego-sense settles is more 'simple', one is tempted to say more 'beautiful'. Out of death comes more perfect life. This sentiment that a higher state of being emerges from death takes us into a crucial area of human creativity.

Reanney continues on the theme of creativity, quoting the psychologist Rollo May. The quote ends with these words:

> Our sense of identity is threatened: the world is not as we experienced it before, and since self and world are always correlated, we are no longer what we were before.

Reanney then picks up this point in respect of grieving:

> This deep insight puts death into an entirely
> different perspective. It is the hallmark of a truly
> creative thought or act that it generates novelty;
> something that was not present before emerges
> from the chaos of creation is caught by the memory
> of the universe. This new insight, this unexpected
> music, inevitably has to destroy the old thought
> forms which it replaces because new symmetries are
> almost invariably moulded from the broken-down
> modules of old assumptions. Death is forever present
> at the cutting edge of consciousness for death is
> the midwife of creative change, of transcendence.
> Always.

Dr Carl Jung (1961) is the earliest writer I have selected; his thought continues to be of huge influence in many areas of life. I love his idea of belief in the hereafter being hygienic, but the statement was typical of all his work. He always saw things from the point of view of psyche and sometimes his explanations foxed both scientists and theologians. He always maintained a strict scientific approach to his work, though this often meant something different to him and took him far from the mainstream. Famously, in his last interview he was asked if he believed in God and his answer was, "No, I don't believe. I know". But what he meant by that was something of a conundrum and certainly not what Christian orthodoxy means by the knowledge of God.

In 1933 Jung published the book which probably had the most popular impact of all his writing, *Modern Man in Search of a Soul*, in this work he states:

> As a physician I am convinced that it is hygienic – if I may use the word- to discover in death a goal towards which one can strive; and that shrinking away from it is something unhealthy and abnormal which robs the second half of life of its purpose. I therefore consider the religious teaching of a life hereafter consonant with the standpoint of psychic hygiene....From the standpoint of psychotherapy it would therefore be desirable to think of death as only a transition – one part of a life-process whose extent and duration escape our knowledge.

Towards the end of his life in his autobiography, *Memories, Dreams, Reflections,* he considers the human tendency to wonder about the life to come and the other tendency, to be prejudiced about what we do not understand:

> It is not that I wish we had a life after death, in fact I would prefer not to foster such ideas. Still, I must state, to give reality its due, that without my wishing and without my doing anything about it, thoughts of this nature move about within me. I can't say whether these thoughts are true or false, but I do know they are there and can be given utterance, if I do not repress them out of some prejudice. Prejudice cripples and injures the full phenomenon of psychic life. And I know too little about psychic life to feel that I can set it right by superior knowledge. Critical rationalism has apparently eliminated, along with

so many other mythic conceptions, the idea of life after death. This could only have happened because nowadays most people identify themselves almost exclusively with their consciousness, and imagine that they are only what they know about themselves. Yet anyone with even a smattering of psychology can see how limited this knowledge is. Rationalism and doctrinairism are the diseases of our time; they pretend to have all the answers. But a great deal will yet be discovered which our present limited view would have ruled out as impossible. Our concepts of space and time have only approximate validity, and there is therefore a wide field for minor and major deviations. In view of all this, I lend an attentive ear to the strange myths of the psyche, and take a careful look at the varied events that come my way, regardless of whether or not they fit in with my theoretical postulates.

There are only two ways to live your life. One is as though nothing is a miracle. The other is as if everything is.

Albert Einstein

My third author is very recent, Dr Eben Alexander, he used the above quote of Einstein in his book *Proof of Heaven*, published in 2012, and it was surely apt for the story he had to tell. Dr Alexander is a highly regarded neuro-physicist who held sensible, scientific views on touchy subjects like near death experiences (NDE's). He is very clear at the start of his book that he knew all the answers from the perspective of someone who was right up to date with the latest research. However, all this was thrown over when he suffered an extended time in a coma. During this period he had extraordinary experiences of Other Dimensions which he remembered with complete lucidity when he regained consciousness. He knew, because he experienced, how vast is the Unseen World.

His story is quite extraordinary and perhaps the most significant fact is that he was a man who knew all the answers, scientifically, to refute any possibility of the continuation of life after physical death. After his experience his view was completely reversed. He came to believe that spirituality cannot afford to be left out of scientific discussion. He saw his journey as pointing to a greater understanding of the very meaning of existence and believed this journey was given to him because his previous training and knowledge was so contrary to what he eventually came to understand, therefore, his testimony would bear more weight.

Another, very beautiful, book is called *Testimony of Light*. This is about two women, Helen and Frances, who had a deep spiritual friendship until Frances' death in 1965. Shortly after her death their communication was resumed; this book is the record of their conversations. It begins quite unexpectedly when Helen was sitting at home one Sunday night and became aware of a Presence and a great stillness into which she felt 'caught up' and drawn into a deep meditative state. Beauty seems to be one of the most significant aspects of her initial experience when she became aware that her friend was with her and wanting to share some soul-level communication. In this way Helen discovers what Frances had always taught, that psychic and spiritual communication are different levels of the same process.

Frances shared with Helen some remarkable information about life in her renewed state and Helen faithfully recorded all that she was given. It was not a long lasting series of talks and in due time Frances came no more. But it was enough to convince Helen of the reality of her friend's ongoing existence and most importantly she gained the recognition that all things are One, in this life and the next. Separation is an illusion of our restricted view, 'not being far enough up the mountain'.

There are various published accounts of people's experiences of Life beyond death, some from Near Death Experiencers, others, as with the two demonstrated here, by people who have in different ways found the means to communicate something of their ineffable experience. Of course each of us will be selective and have our personal criteria for deciding about authenticity. I find myself most convinced not just by sincerity but by a certain sense of reverence and holiness, though I confess I am swayed when an account somehow accords with my personal hopes, desires or expectations!

> What we call the beginning is often the end
> And to make an end is to make a beginning.
> The end is where we start from.

T.S.Eliot: Four Quartets Little Gidding V

In conclusion I must say a few words about T.S. Eliot's poetry, particularly *Four Quartets*, which has been quoted often throughout this collection. Eliot's poetry illuminates our inner experiences, creates meanings and gives us the words for what it is beyond us to express. If you are new to it, initially, it may be hard work; some of it is obscure, but like all good poetry, the more often you read it the more the meaning opens up. And, as we have seen, we do not have to grasp at meaning but allow the words to work for us. In fact, 'What it all means' is a theme running through the whole poem:

> We had the experience but missed the meaning,
> And approach to the meaning restores the
> > experience
> In a different form, beyond any meaning
> We can assign to happiness.

Dry Salvages II

This time in grief's hermitage is a time of beginning, but we start from the end; from the end of the life we knew and the beginning of something as yet unknown. Time, beginning, ending and most particularly 'The point of intersection of the timeless/with time,' (which is the apprehension of Eternity) are the recurring themes which Eliot is exploring throughout the poem.

The *Quartets* ends with the now very familiar quote from Mother Julian of Norwich, a Fourteenth Century English hermit. Julian was writing at the time of the Black Death, so she knew a great deal about suffering and grief, nevertheless she could still claim the all would be well; a fitting reassurance for this present time in our own hermitage.

> A condition of complete simplicity
> (Costing not less than everything)
> And all shall be well and
> All manner of things shall be well
> When the tongues of flame are in-folded

Into the crowned knot of fire
And the fire and the rose are one.

AFTERWORD

Living alone there will always be days,
Early evening, last thing at night,
First thing in the morning,
When everyone is elsewhere,
in their customary place,
Doing their customary thing,
with the people they love.
You are solitary.
No touch, no laughter, no inconsequential chat.

You can please yourself what you eat.
Having no-one else to please
Eating is just a bore
Necessary but dull.
One solution is to 'get on'.
Being busy takes your mind off the problem
Or making a call:
Find or phone a friend
To dull the pain.
Read a book, watch the tele, or, more sinister,
Take the discomfort into the realm
of physical problems.
"What's the matter with me?
I don't feel at all well.
There must be something wrong
And it might be serious.
Perhaps I should see someone."
'Someone' will take this seriously
Advise many tests and explorations

But there is no test that reveals
The seat of loneliness.
The source is a perfectly
Functioning heart.
These are all distractions.
They come and go.

Attend, accept consciously
With full awareness.
I am well, I am grateful
And I am aching with
Perfectly normal, human needs
Unmet.

MORE OF HERMITS
AND HERMITAGE

This chapter is just a little more on the background meaning of the
ideas that have in the past attached to hermits. It may be of interest
to people who enjoy delving into the symbolic meaning of things.

As we saw, the idea of a hermit was attached to the women and men
who wanted a life set apart. The word comes from the Greek word
for desert, *eremos*, which is where the hermits tended to hang out.
The derivation of the idea, though, goes back even further, back into
the realm of the Greek gods.

Hermes was the god of luck and wealth, and patron of merchants
and thieves, but he was also a fertility god and the god of the roads.
It was Hermes who conducted the souls of the dead into the Nether
Regions; he was the messenger of the gods and the god of sleep and
dreams. It is easy to see universal or Archetypal themes here that
can inform our process though we may not envision the inspiration
as a Greek god. We may recognise the sacred, an angel or some
aspect of the Divine; we might simply call it an Energy. However we
chose to name it, it is comforting to trust that the Divine, in some
form, watches over our sleep and dreams and hovers over the road
we must take. If we are listening, there may be intimations from the

Other Realm, a whisper of something more than the mere dreary everydayness. This seclusion, if one separates off from outside influences, can be fertile and calming.

Digging even deeper, behind the fairly straightforward Hermes as messenger of the gods we come upon Hermes Trismegistus, which is a name to conjure with, meaning 'thrice greatest Hermes'. The title comes from an assortment of texts, believed by the ancient Greeks to go back to the early Egyptians. These texts carried deep religious significance and have been discovered and re-discovered many times in the history of the human search for the divine. Some of the early Christian writers loved these writings and wanted to prove that, as all things came from the One True God, the texts must originally have come from Moses!

Wherever it comes from, some of the material in the Hermetic Books is comforting to ponder from the hermitage, if you are willing to take the symbolic view. For example, in ancient Egypt it was thought that the soul is a union of light and life; that nothing is destructible and that suffering is the result of motion. So being still and trusting that "all things exist and ever shall exist because that God loveth them" maybe a word of comfort in our dark hours.

For the ancient devotee the seclusion and separation led to the experience of rebirth; for us, too, the stillness and the separation within our hermitage can evolve into the experience of re-birth. We can no longer be the person we were because that person comprised, also, the intertwining with the beloved, the loved one gone, we have to be re-configured, and ultimately we are re-born.

Many ancient cultures believed that God (in the case of the Jews) or the gods spoke to people in dreams. Analytical psychology through the work of giants like Sigmund Freud and Carl Jung has, over the last century or so, restored this facility to us. The language may have changed and the explanations given a scientific veneer, but whether you call their source the Unconscious or God or the gods, dreams are considered by many to bring information, cryptically, from beyond our daily consciousness. The dreams we have when we have lost someone we love can be a very meaningful guide, provided, of course, that we understand that the language of dreams is not the language of every day. In dreams we are here in the land of symbols, *where things are never what they seem.*

One last word on the hermetic tradition: alchemy. Alchemy was the earliest form of scientific enquiry. The alchemist researched into the nature of things and engaged with the process of transmutation, that is, to change a substance into a superior form. This was a serious religious quest that required great concentration and severe discipline. The core idea was to turn base metal into gold. For this they used a large vessel with a close fitting lid; once the process was set in motion the lid was fitted and not lifted until the work was complete. This pot was called 'the Hermetic vessel'.

The symbolic significance of this endeavour is what makes it interesting because the real quest was to turn the 'base metal' of human bodily existence into the 'gold' of a fully conscious spiritual person. Today, the process of psycho-analysis is often referred to as the Hermetic vessel and clients are advised, to 'keep the lid on' the work they are doing, i.e. not to talk about what goes on during sessions. This is another aspect of outside influences which can deflect us from our real purpose; other people's opinions can sway us, especially when we are lost or not sure of where we are going. In our hermitage, which is our Hermetic vessel, the base metal of our suffering and grief is being transmuted into the gold of new life and that takes time, not knowing, silence and trust. Patiently, it may be necessary to:

> and wait without hope
> For hope would be hope for the wrong thing; wait without
> > love
> For love would be love of the wrong thing; there is yet
> > faith
> But the faith and the love and the hope are all in the
> > waiting.
> Wait without thought, for you are not ready for
> > thought:
> So the darkness shall be the light, and the stillness the
> > dancing.

T.S. Eliot: Four Quartets East Coker III

ACKNOWLEDGEMENTS

Ednah St Vincent Millay 'Time Does Not Bring Relief" and 'Dirge Without Music' is included by kind permission of The Millay Society.

Vera Brittain's 'Perhaps' is included by permission of Mark Bostridge and T.J. Brittain-Catlin, Literary Executors for the Vera Brittain Estate.

Frances Cornford. 'The Watcher' and 'Afterthought' From Collected Poems Published by Barrie & Jenkins. Reproduced by permission of The Random House Group Ltd.

Coward© Noel Coward, 'When I Have Fears', from 'The Complete Verse of Noel Coward', by kind permission of Bloomsbury Methuen Drama, an imprint of Bloomsbury Publishing Plc.

Mary Dilworth 'Grief' and 'Just Another Death' from An Anthology of Christian Verse (Sydney 1983 edited by Francis Byrne O.S.B.) by kind permission of the author.

Eliot T.S.Eliot   'The Journey of the Magi' and 'Four Quartets'.

from The Complete Poems and Plays (London 1977) by kind permission of Faber and Faber publishers.

Kathleen Raine 'Spell Against Sorrow' from Selected Poems by permission of the Literary Estate of Kathleen Raine.

Edward Thomas 'Liberty'. Though this poet is out of copyright I'd like to acknowledge the kind co-operation of Mr Colin Thornton of The Edward Thomas fellowship.

R.S. Thomas 'But silence in the mind....' From Collected Later Poems 1988-2000 (Bloodaxe Books, 2004) reproduced with permission of Bloodaxe Books on behalf of the Estate of R.S.Thomas.

R.S Thomas "The Arrival" from Collected Poems 1945-1900 by permission from The Orion Publishing group, London (copyright R.S.Thomas 1993).

GRIEF'S HERMITAGE

Dereck Walcott 'Love after Love' from Poems 1965-1980 (London 1992) by kind permission of Faber and Faber publishers.

C.S.Lewis A Grief Observed (London 1961)by kind permission of Faber and Faber publishers.

I offer my sincere apologies for not being able to make proper acknowledgements for the following two titles. Every effort has been made, without success, to trace the present owners of the copyrights and I will gladly remedy this in future editions if the proper authority can be found.

Darryl Reanney The Death of Forever (Melbourne 1991).

Stephen Verney Into the New Age (London 1976).

My thanks to Ms Katie Pelosi for preparing the initial design for the book and cover and to Julie-Anne Harper and her staff at the Pick-a-woo-woo Publishing Group. All these people are not only professional in their approach but kind, patient and enduring with an author who remains something of a Luddite when it comes to electronic technology.

My daughters are unfailingly kind and supportive, I owe them a great deal. They gave me the support and enthusiasm without which this book would not have seen the light of day. Happily, Bronwen Joy's proof reading skills ensured that it arrived free from many blips and blemishes with which it started out.

SELECTED BIBLIOGRAPHY

Abbe de Tourville	Letters of Direction (London 1939)
Alexander, Eben	Proof of Heaven (New York 2012)
Bloom, Harold (ed)	Till I End My Song (New York 2010)
Brontë Sisters	Poems (Folio, London 1987)
Brooke, Rupert	Poetical Work (London 1946)
Browning, Elizabeth Barrett	Poems (London 1998)
Bullett, Gerald (ed)	The English Galaxy of Shorter Poems (London 1947)
Byrne, Francis O.S.B. (ed)	An Anthology of Christian Verse (Sydney 1983)
Caudwell, Sarah	The Shortest Way to Hades (New York 1985)
Coward, Noel	The Complete Verse (London Folio 1996)
Donne, John	The Complete English Poems (Folio, London 2005)
Eliot, T.S.	The Complete Poems and Plays (London 1977)
Enright D.J. (ed)	The Oxford Book of Death (Oxford 1983)
Greaves, Helen	Testimony of Light (Bury St. Edmunds 1969)
Hardy, Thomas	Poems (London 1974)
Heath-Stubbs, John and Wright, David (eds)	The Faber Book of Twentieth Century Verse (London 1953)

Hill, Reginald	The Spy's Wife (London 1980)
Jerome K. Jerome	Three Men in a Boat (London 1889)
Johnson, William	Silent Music (Glasgow 1976)
Jung, C.G.	Modern Man in Search of a Soul (London 1933) Memories, Dreams, Reflections (London 1967)
Keynes, Geoffrey (ed)	The Poetical Works of Rupert Brooke (London 1946)
Larkin, Philip (ed)	The Oxford Book of Twentieth Century English Verse (London 1973)
Lewis, C.S.	A Grief Observed (London 1961)
May. G. Lacey (ed)	English Religious Verse (London 1950)
Milford, H.S. (ed)	The Oxford Book of English Romantic Verse (Oxford 1935)
Nouwen, Henri J.M.	Reaching Out (London 1976)
Raine, Kathleen	Selected Poems (Lindisfarne 1988)
Reanney, Darryl	The Death of Forever (London 1991)
Shakespeare, William	Collected Works
Studdert-Kennedy G.A.	The Unutterable Beauty (London 1947)
Synge, J.M.	Plays, Poems and Prose (London 1941)
Tagore, Rabindranath	Collected Poems and Plays (London 1977)
Tennyson, Alfred, Lord	Poetical Works (London, undated)
Thomas R.S.	Collected Poems 1945-1990 (London 1993)
Thomas, R.S.	Collected Later Poems 1988 – 2000 (Northumberland 2004)
Walcott, Dereck	Poems 1965-1980 (London 1992)
Wordsworth, William	Selected Poems (Folio, London 2002)

Printed in Australia
AUOC02n1415110118
293506AU00001B/1/P

9 780648 169703